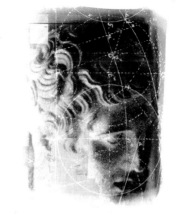

are you
psychic?

are you
psychic?

dozens of
TECHNIQUES
for boosting your innate powers

Julie Soskin

CARROLL & BROWN PUBLISHERS LIMITED

First published in 2002 in the United Kingdom by:

CARROLL & BROWN LIMITED
20 Lonsdale Road
London NW6 6RD

Editor **Yvonne Deutsch**
Art Editor **Gilda Pacitti**
Designer **Evie Loizides-Graham**
Photographer **Jules Selmes**

Text copyright © Julie Soskin 2002
Compilation © Carroll & Brown Limited 2002

A catalogue record for this book is available from the British Library

ISBN 1-903258-20-0
Reproduced by Colourscan, Singapore
Printed and bound in Singapore by Imago
First Edition

Contents

Introduction

People often refer to "gut feelings, or instincts." This is a sense of knowing that cannot easily be rationally expressed or intellectually confirmed. People are often heard to say things like, "I knew I should have done that" and there is usually an overriding feeling of something being either right or wrong, without having a specific reason for it. Where does this feeling come from? Is there an innate psychic or intuitive faculty from which we could all benefit? How do we access it? And if we do so, why won't we trust this extra sense which is often referred to as the sixth sense?

Throughout this book we will investigate how much you use your psychic senses and how you might further train any psychic potentials. Taking the mystical view that we all possess divinity within, is it possible for us all to tap into higher awareness, to tune into information beyond normal means?

Many people regard the very notion of being psychic as something that belongs at a fairground. But most people, at some time in their lives, have consulted their horoscopes in the papers, or read some of the increasing number of articles or books on affiliated subjects, or even have been to some form of psychic or medium. Over the last twenty years, there has been massive interest in psychic and spiritual topics, so much so that psychism has emerged from the secular into the main stream. Why then is there so much interest in this age-old subject?

To access psychic information, the seeker needs to be a clear instrument, which often necessitates some kind of self-development or transformative process. Psychic refers to an unseen force; it derives from the word psyche, which means of, or pertaining to, the soul, mind, or spirit. In the allegorical Greek story of the mortal princess, Psyche, she had to endure many tests and trials to prove herself worthy of being the companion of the god of love, Eros. When at last she is given the cup of immortality, she sprouts butterfly wings, which are ancient symbols of the soul. This story suggests that in seeking unconditional love, we, too, might be transformed.

Perhaps one of our greatest attributes is our curiosity, our desire to learn, to make our existence a life-long learning venture. In this book we shall explore some interesting questions about who we are and whether we are psychic and, if so, how we can enlarge and possibly use any psychic talents we may possess.

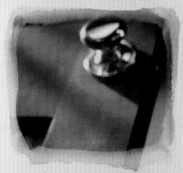

We will explore avenues of sensitivity, to help you assess how much you can rely on your inner knowing, to aid you in your own voyage of discovery. What you ultimately do about your gifts only you can decide. Anyone with ten fingers on his or her hands, with enough dedication and perseverance could learn how to play a tune on the piano. Few, however, will become concert pianists. Psychic abilities could be seen in the same way; anyone with a strong desire to use these attributes will be able to access his or her intuition, very few are able, or indeed would want, to work as a professional in the field.

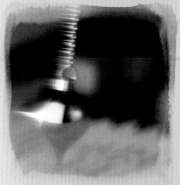

Are You Psychic? is laid out for inter-active exchange. It contains simple questionnaires and exercises that will immediately give you some feedback about your approach to and potential success in the various areas of psychism. Often, there are suggestions about strengthening your "gifts" using the exercises and practices in the book. If the process of discovery is successful, you should be able to use your intuition in beneficial ways in your day-to-day life. You will be able to see for yourself how a new perspective can aid you in not only being conscious of what's around you now, but also help you take charge of your own destiny.

The first chapter of *Are You Psychic?* helps you discover any latent psychic talents and develop your psychic potential. How intuitive are you? Are your senses sufficiently awakened? Do you understand your will and use positive thought? Can you exert mind over matter? The chapter also provides you with insight into how meditation, sharpening your psychic vision, and comprehending the chakras and auras can lead to profound discoveries.

The next chapter tackles Extra-Sensory Perceptions. Is it possible to read minds? Travel to places without leaving your armchair? Look into the future? Or decipher dreams that inform you of your needs?

Chapter three considers the psychic aids at your disposal. Astrology, the I Ching, Tarot, Scrying, Palm Reading and Divining — all can provide insights that no other form of communication can.

Chapter four is concerned with spiritual healing and with simple approaches to balancing energies for health and well being. Does the body speak to us through illness and if so can we do something to heal ourselves? Can you sufficiently develop your innate powers so that you can heal not only yourself but others? Readers will be advised on using particular "tools" such as crystals, music, and color. This section ends with glorious color pages, which not only inform, but can be used for meditation and healing purposes.

Chapter five looks at communication with non-physical beings. Have you ever encountered a ghost? Are there such things as poltergeists? And do angels really help us throughout our lives? Could you be a shaman, someone who allows spirits of nature to talk through you, or become closer to a spirit guide?

The penultimate section covers psychic protection. If you are looking at developing your intuitive powers, you need to be discerning and protected. Some psychic self defense is used in part five to aid you through your progress. Finally, in the last chapter, I discuss the implications of beginning to see the world through higher levels of consciousness. How can you best channel these energies and does karma really work within our lives? What is the transpersonal self and can it assist the function of our intuition effectively?

In entering the psychic world, people often lose sight of the joy of living and the fun of the adventure. In this book, I hope to inject some enjoyment into the crucial subject of how we manage psychic forces in our lives, and what we therefore may achieve.

Keeping a Psychic Journal

One of the best the ways to develop your psychic skills is to record your insights, ideas, dreams, and observations in a special notebook. This can help train you to be increasingly self-aware and will provide you with a reference base to help you to keep track of your progress and problems. You might like to start by asking yourself the questions set out on page 11 in order to direct your psychic growth. There could be things on the list that you are trying to overcome, achieve, or improve. Keep the notebook by your bedside; this way you can record whatever dreams you have (page 66) as well as your day-time thoughts. Before going to sleep each night, review the day's events, recalling not just your own feelings and experiences, but the reactions of others. Avoid getting caught up in the emotions of any situation—stay objective. Keep asking yourself questions. How do people respond to you and what energy from you attracts that response? Be honest in your assessment—that way you'll achieve the necessary overview for success in psychic work.

The golden rules

Write the following guidelines in your journal as a constant reminder to use your psychic abilities ethically and responsibly:

Never offer psychic insights unless asked for them.

Don't exaggerate your psychic capabilities.

Under no circumstances manipulate or control others.

Never tell someone when or how you think he or she will die.

Avoid judging or condemning someone else's behavior.

Journal notes: Food for thought

One very good reason to develop your psychic abilities is because they may be able to change your life for the better. Therefore, you should give some thought as to what needs changing. The questions below are really prompts to start you thinking about your ultimate goal(s).

- What have you always wanted?
- What gives or will give you the most pleasure?
- What do you spend your time thinking/wishing about most?
- What behavior in others do you most admire but feel is lacking in yourself?
- Is there anything that you were deprived of as a child that you still yearn for?
- Is there a difference between the things/people you value and the things you think most about—and how do you go about changing this?
- What are your priorities? What are you doing about them?
- What beliefs would help you to experience more fun, trust and joy? And help you deal with anger, fear, and grief?
- What is preventing you from making the necessary changes to become the person you really want to be?

DISCOVER YOUR PSYCHIC POTENTIAL

1

How Intuitive Are You?

Intuitive intelligence is a valuable tool for living. Your "sixth sense" gives you access to information that seems to come from nowhere, but is often uncannily accurate. There are various theories about how this happens. You could see it as your mind drawing together everything that it knows and coming up with the right answer from your personal, instant-access database.

A psychic might regard intuition as the ability to go beyond individual experience, tapping into much broader sources, similar to plugging into the world-wide web. Like most people, you already have some intuitive ability, but there are positive ways to develop this even further. Many of the exercises in this book—particularly meditation (see page 22)—are specially designed to help you to achieve the concentrated inner focus that will help you to recognize messages from your inner self.

The exercises can also give you more confidence in yourself, and enable you not only to trust your intuition but to act on it. This is particularly helpful if you often doubt your perceptions, and explain away your intuitive insights with "rational" explanations. The best way to overcome this barrier is to take a mental "leap" into the unknown. This means suspending all assumptions, bias and prejudices, and learning to be open to the promptings of your psychic sensitivity. This will open up a whole new resource of vision, and make you much more sure in your judgment; you'll be able to see through surface detail, and make fast, accurate decisions in any situation.

Intuition boosters

Even if you regard yourself as a very analytical person, you can still enhance your intuition.

Instead of dismissing any insights you have about people or events that seem to defy logic, start paying attention to these, and record them in your psychic journal.

If you ever get a sudden sense of danger or threat, never ignore it—trust your intuition.

Learn to identify your sharp, rationalizing "voice." If you hear yourself saying "nonsense" when you can't explain something that's bothering you, that's when you should listen to your soft, persistent, intuitive "voice."

If one of your hidden feelings, hunches or predictions is proved right, enjoy the feeling of being "right on" in your judgment, and make a note whenever this happens.

Be playful with your intuition: create harmless "games"—for instance, imagine what someone is about to say, or what they'll wear tomorrow.

Do you have a sixth sense?

If you respond "yes" to a question, check the box next to it. Add up the checks and note your score.

❏ Have you instantly felt that a building was a happy or threatening place?

❏ Do you "know" that you can or can't trust someone?

❏ When the phone rings, do you often know who is calling?

❏ Can you "hear" someone's thoughts and verbalize them?

❏ Have you ever had a physical sensation of someone walking through you?

❏ When looking for a parking space, have you ever followed your instinct to turn down an unfamiliar road, and then found a space?

❏ When you wake up, do you feel something has been revealed to you during the night?

❏ While talking to a person you've never met before, have you ever had a compelling feeling that something unpleasant would happen to him or her? And have you been told later that the person had been in an accident or had become ill?

❏ When you close your eyes do you sometimes see eyes or human faces?

❏ Do the hairs on the back of your neck sometimes bristle, putting you on your guard?

❏ Have you ever made a decision against the advice of friends and family, just because it felt right?

❏ Are you someone who experiences an unusual number of coincidences?

How many questions did you check?

❏ 1–2
Even if you ticked just one or two boxes, you have some access to your intuitive resources—and these can be developed.

❏ 3–5
Your intuition is quite active, but you have room to improve. Learn to trust yourself and let your instinct guide you.

❏ 7–9
You're already well tuned in to your inner sources of wisdom—and with practice, you can use intuition even more precisely.

❏ 10 or over
Your intuitive abilities are powerfully developed and you have the confidence to trust your innate judgement.

What Kind of Psychic Are You?

You can be psychic in different ways. For instance, intuitive empaths have a great understanding of what is going on with others but may have little sensitivity to atmosphere. Those with shamanic abilities derive a special energy from communicating with nature spirits and are gifted healers—but they may not be drawn to psychic tools such as tarot cards or runes. Mediums have the ability to link with spirits, but unlike channelers, may not be able to connect with higher spiritual forces. Use the questionnaire opposite to discover *your* psychic style.

Identifying your skills

Give the following questions careful thought, then check *only* those to which you have an affirmative response.

❏ **1**   Are you generally aware of other people's feelings?

❏ **2**   Do you ever get a sense that you are part of the universe?

❏ **3**   Do you often know what other people will say before they say it?

❏ **4**   While walking outdoors have you sensed something watching you?

❏ **5**   Out in open country, have you felt something did not want you there?

❏ **6**   Have you been out in a wild space and felt the place protected you?

Assessment

Look at your final total of "yes" answers. Do all, or most of them, fit into one of the following groups of numbers? If so, this will give you a good idea of what kind of psychic you are most likely to be.

1 3 7 8 12
You are an EMPATH

The ability to literally feel for someone else is a finely tuned empathic sense. It gives you the psychic ability to "read" a person's aura, and interpret the information back to him or her (see page 42). It can bring you amazingly close to others; you can sense their true emotional needs with unerring accuracy, and people may be drawn to you like magnets. But avoid absorbing other people's problems, as it's easy to get burned out.

❏ 7 Do you get butterflies in your stomach when you are near someone?

❏ 8 Do you get the same butterfly feeling in a location?

❏ 9 When you walk into a place for the first time can you sense the atmosphere?

❏ 10 Do you really know that the world could be a place of peace and love instead of starvation and wars?

❏ 11 Have you walked into a place and felt a shiver or a sense of a presence?

❏ 12 Do you ever "hear" people's thoughts?

❏ 13 Are there people that you do not like to be physically near?

❏ 14 Have you had an encounter with a spirit of any kind?

❏ 15 Have you woken up to feel a weight on you when nothing physical is there?

❏ 16 Do you get a sense of wonder and love just by being alive?

❏ 17 Do you have vivid dreams that you feel may have really happened?

❏ 18 Do you look into the eyes of someone who is hurting you and see their pain?

❏ 19 At night do you close your eyes and see eyes, faces or human-like creatures?

❏ 20 Have you felt your body has been on a journey without you moving?

2 10 16 18
You are a CHANNELER

Accessing information and/or energy from a higher level of consciousness is often called channeling (see page 168). There is no sense of contact with an individual entity, rather, a connection to higher spiritual forces. Whatever your age, you are viewed by others as "an old soul" and will be sought out for the spiritual insight that you've built up over many lifetimes.

11 14 15 17 19 20
You are a MEDIUM

If you've been aware of an unseen presence, or have seen a ghost, you could be mediumistic (see page 142). You also may have felt the presence of angelic or earthly spirits, which act as guardians to you. You can look into other dimensions such as the astral worlds or the "spirit" world. This vision is a rare gift.

4 5 6 9 13
You are a SHAMAN

As you are vividly aware of nature and the spirit in animals, plants and trees, your style of psychism is shamanistic (see page 140). You derive a highly tuned sense of danger from your instinctive link with wild animals; this is a great asset—your intuition literally saves lives. You can sense impending danger in all situations, whether it's on the sidewalk, in traffic situations, or in the workplace. You may also have natural healing ability—an innate sense of what will harm or help someone who is ill.

Awaken Your Senses

Psychic sensitivity is not based on some obscure formula known to a few privileged people; on the contrary, you already have every ingredient you need in your five senses. Every second of the day, you're absorbing a changing blend of aromas, flavors, sounds, sights, and textures. The process is so automatic it's easy to take it for granted but without your senses you would literally be "dead" to the world. This is the polar opposite of a psychic's experience of life, where everything is vivid, sensuous, and alive with meaning.

People who are unusually sensitive can perceive atmospheres, feel invisible presences, see visions, hear messages, and experience reality on many different levels. With a little practice, you'll be able to do all this yourself.

A Day of Vision

Ideally, you should choose a day that has a full moon on the same evening (see the exercise opposite). As soon as you wake up, tell yourself out loud: "Today I am going to look closely at everything around me."

Journal notes: Five sensational days

- Exploring your senses to their limits takes time, space, and imagination. It also requires the ability to focus: a simple way to achieve this is to allot an entire day to discovering a single sense. Then, at the end of that day, write up your experiences in your psychic journal.

- Note down your reactions to any incident, exercise or experiment that gave you positive feedback, and made an active difference to your sensory awareness.

- Pay attention to the exact quality of your reactions; notice whether you felt excited, calmed, aroused, amused, inspired; or frightened, uneasy, curious, or repelled.

- Each day's events may also trigger a special chain of association in your mind: for example, a fleeting scent, a fading color, a grain of wood—any of these can release a flood of memories.

- You may remember people and places that you had long forgotten. Again, write everything down; all these links will lead you toward enhanced psychic awareness.

CANDLE-GAZING

How to enhance your psychic sight.

1 *Choose a quiet, dimly lit place, and light a candle. Place it on a table, and sit down, facing the candle. Get yourself quietly relaxed.*

2 *Gaze into the candle flame, staying relaxed and calm, watching the flame.*

3 *Now, focus your gaze at the place where the blue color of the flame meets with the gold—this is the point where your potential for psychic sight can be developed. Continue gazing at this spot until you feel you have absorbed enough.*

This triggers your visual awareness and prepares your intuition for action. As you go through your day, look at everything with the candid gaze of a child—try to see things just as they are. Look at objects, buildings, colors, people's faces, animals, and plants with new eyes. Don't spend time "evaluating" —simply look. This way, you'll take in more visual messages, as you won't be censoring or rejecting anything. At some point in the day, try one of the "gazing" exercises described below.

A Day to Follow Your Nose

The moment you wake up, say out loud: "Today I am going to experience as many different smells as possible." This message will literally put you on the scent; follow your nose through the day, and notice every aroma—starting with the smells of your morning toast and coffee. Be alert to everything— fumes from traffic; smells from coffee shops and restaurants; the waft of perfume from a passer-by. Sniff your newspaper, and breathe in the smell of a leather wallet. This prepares your psychic antennae

MOON-GAZING

See a new vision in the full moon.

1 *Find a quiet place to relax and look up at the full moon; allow your gaze to become completely absorbed by the moon's light.*

2 *Next, close your eyes, and note the intense blue image imprinted on your retina. Draw this blue color toward you, and use it to visualize yourself.*

3 *If there is no full moon, you could try gazing briefly into a 100 watt light bulb; but you should never look into the full glare of the sun, as this could damage your eyesight.*

for action, as the first hint of an invisible presence may be a certain smell. A faint, old-fashioned scent could be a link with a departed grandmother, and a pungent whiff of tobacco may announce a man who always had a pipe with him when he was alive.

A Day to Listen Closely

Your wake-up message for your listening day says: "Today I'll keep my ears open and hear what the world really sounds like." You may think this is easy; but you're probably unaware of how much sound you automatically block out. This form of "natural selection" is a survival mechanism, helping you to focus on the important signals around you. One of the first signs of stress is the inability to cope with a constant bombardment of grating and discordant sounds, and censoring these helps you to stay calm and balanced. You can use a consciously selective approach and focus on different sounds, as if they were separate notes in a piece of music. Turn the day into your private musical with tunes made up from varying notes: automobile horns; ringing telephones; beeping vehicles; hissing coffee machines; clacking cups and saucers; whirring elevators; a slammed door; sudden shrieks; barks; and laughter.

WHAT'S THAT SMELL?

This exercise can be very revealing.

1 *Ask a close friend to make up a "sampler" tray: it could include things like a lemon; furniture polish; starch; stationery; spices; mothballs; a smelly insole; and an overripe piece of cheese.*

2 *Keep your eyes closed or blindfolded, and smell each item individually. Take time to experience each scent—it's just as important to identify what feelings are evoked in you as it is to identify the source of the smell.*

LISTEN TO THE BIRDS

Here's how to follow each part of a symphony of bird song.

1 *Find an outdoor space, where there are plenty of birds—this could be a public park or in your garden.*

2 *Sit quietly relaxed, listening to the medley of birdsong around you. At some point you'll distinguish one song from the others. Focus on this, and spend time listening to it.*

3 *Now let the song of this bird take you to another's, and listen to this for a while. Again, you'll find that you're naturally drawn to the next bird in line. Listen intuitively to each song, sensing the essence within each.*

A Touchy-Feely Day

In the morning, look at yourself in the bathroom mirror and announce: "Today I will live each moment through my hands." Let your fingers tingle in anticipation and start from home: run your hands over the surface of your skin and through your hair; feel your bath towel; touch the cool porcelain of your bathtub; note the slick sensation of a plastic toy; and feel the bristles of your toothbrush with your fingertips. Throughout the day, make a point of touching as many different textures as possible—smooth, furry, silken, rough, warm, cold—and notice all the different sensations you experience, both positive and negative.

Tasting the Day

If you like eating and drinking, you'll probably enjoy spending an entire day in an extended tasting session. But you should still alert your taste buds first thing in the morning by saying: "Today I'll pay close attention to everything that I taste." This starts from the moment the flavor of toothpaste floods your mouth; you may follow that with a swirl of mouthwash. What do these flavors evoke? Cool mints? Spicy cloves? Cinnamon? Consider the flavor of everything you put in your mouth. And explore unfamiliar things—for example, if you want to give your taste buds a real shock, touch the end of your tongue with a metal coin.

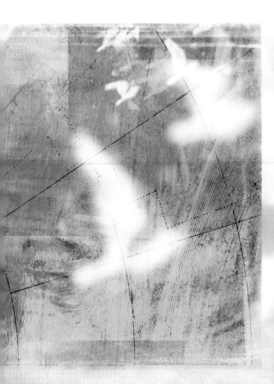

A GUIDED TOUR

This journey starts with a simple touch.

1 *Ask someone who knows you well to pick out a distinctively textured object for you.*

2 *Close your eyes and ask your friend to place the item in your hands; as you explore it, talk about the places it evokes. It may take you into a garden from childhood; onto a beach; or somewhere you've never been before.*

3 *Visualize yourself there. Explore your surroundings thoroughly and pay attention to everything that you see. If there are people or animals, how do you feel about them? When you've completely absorbed the feeling of the place, open your eyes.*

DISCRIMINATING TASTE

Use this subtle method to tune your senses and taste the air around you.

1 *Sit in a quiet, airy place and use the breathing method on page 23 to get yourself deeply relaxed.*

2 *Breathe slowly and regularly, then open your mouth slightly. Let the air around you flow into your mouth.*

3 *Focus on the taste of the air, and open yourself completely to whatever you're sensing. You'll be surprised at how much information you'll receive this way.*

Opening Up through Meditation

If you want to do any form of psychic work, the most important skill to perfect is being able to contact your inner stillness. Whatever your aspirations—to enhance your powers of healing, telepathy, or clairvoyance or to learn how you can view auras or connect with the spirit world—you'll first need to know how to meditate.

If you've never meditated before, you may believe that it is a pleasant way of escaping from the world and its problems. Although it does lead to inner stillness, calm, or "the silent place within," meditation is certainly not just about melting into bliss. Rather, it is a powerful tool to help you focus clearly on your physical being. Just as important, it also puts you directly in touch with universal energy or "prana"—the life force that runs though all things. This level of consciousness is precisely what you need to achieve your psychic ambitions; but it improves your life in other ways, too. Meditation sharpens and focuses your mental activity and keeps

Guidelines to meditation

Find a clean, quiet, airy, comfortable, uncluttered place and dedicate this spot to meditation—working in the same area builds up a positive energy.

Unplug the phone before starting and lock the door if you think you might be disturbed.

Wear comfortable, loose, clean clothing.

Bathe or shower, or at least wash your hands.

You may want to use something to focus your meditation; this can be an object such as a candle, flower, or picture, a sound such as a mantra, or ambient music.

Sit in a chair or on the floor with your back supported. Place your arms on your legs with your hands in an open position—this puts you in the right posture.

Devote your whole attention to your point of focus; start with five minutes then gradually increase the time to twenty, if possible.

Do not force your mind to concentrate. Keep it focused but without effort. When thoughts intrude, don't push them away but let them float by. If your mind wanders, return it to its focus, no matter how often it escapes.

It's a good idea to meditate at the same time every day—many people choose first thing in the morning, as meditation is usually better on an empty stomach. Meditation last thing at night can just cause you to fall asleep, so find a time that suits you to meditate regularly.

you alert at work, at home, and in your relationships. It also enhances creativity and self-knowledge.

Most of the psychic development exercises in this book start by asking you to get into a completely relaxed state, and the meditation technique below is one of the most effective ways of doing this. Once you have become completely familiar with it, you'll have the key to opening yourself up to a completely new world of experiences. This way, meditation will dramatically change your life.

BREATHING IN THE LIGHT

This exercise is the key to complete relaxation; it can last as long or as short a time as you wish.

1 *Work in a quiet room where you feel relaxed. You may want to put on some soothing music to help you wind down. When you are completely calm, turn off the music and concentrate.*

2 *Direct your conscious awareness onto your breathing, and listen attentively.*

3 *Tune into the ebb and flow of your breath, and gently focus onto this quiet rhythm, so that your entire being is at one with your breathing. Take your time while doing this— you are entering a deep meditative state.*

4 *Let your breath take you to your inner calm, the "still place within," and consciously breathe that stillness out from the core of your being.*

5 *Visualize your breathing as ripples on a pond, moving outward in increasingly large circles, or as waves of light radiating from your body.*

6 *Deliberately hold the energy and keep your focus—don't be tempted to "float away." After a while, as you breathe, concentrate on the thought that every living thing breathes. Say to yourself **"We all breathe in light."** Now let yourself become completely open to the universal forces of light. Stay with this feeling as long as you like.*

7 *When you're ready, gently lead your consciousness back into your physical body (paying particular attention to keeping your feet on the ground).*

8 *Finally, cross your arms and legs, as an act of closing.*

Your Inner Quest

To find your real self, you must ask: "Who am I?"
Let your mind confront this. At first you'll think of
yourself in terms of your role in life. Keep asking: Is
this really you? If you persist, you will finally arrive
at the core of your true self, which does not change.

If a question is nagging at your mind, the clarity
you achieve during meditation will assist you. Don't
expect an instant answer—it usually comes when
you least expect it. Meanwhile, meditative energy
will have assessed the question through other
perceptions.

If you have an especially active brain, a "Koan" or
paradoxical statement may help. This is a question
that de-intellectualizes the mind by its lack of logic;
the common Zen example is "What is the sound of
one hand clapping?"

Meditation Pathways

You may need to explore several avenues before
you discover the approach to meditation that works
best for you. Each of the pathways described
opposite offers a slightly different resonance. None
is "better" than the others—they are all simply
alternatives. Whatever route you choose, you'll
intuitively recognize when you've arrived at the
unique, calm center within yourself. This is the
entire point of the journey.

SEEK THE STILL VOICE
*Light, breath, music, and mantras are different points of
focus that you can use during meditation. Choose the one
that brings you to the still voice within yourself.*

Breath

Breathing is the simplest focus, and observing its natural rhythms can help to calm the mind. Let each breath enter and leave your body at its normal pace and observe how it moves and reverberates through your body. If you like, you can count the inhalations and exhalations to assist. Inhale to the count of 1 to 4, pause for a few seconds, then exhale to the count of 1 to 4.

Music

You may find that special meditative music tapes or certain classical pieces can help to clear the mind of intrusive thoughts. If you've never meditated before, music may be just the pathway you need to help you.

Mantra

The repetition of a single sound, word, or phrase produces a powerful force that will block the intrusion of other thoughts. You may wish to focus on a sacred or personally meaningful word. You can say it aloud or repeat it silently. It can be helpful to synchronize your mantra with your breathing, saying it on every out- or in-breath. If your attention wanders, gently bring it back to your mantra.

Light

A lit candle placed in front of you can help work as a point of focus if you prefer to meditate with your eyes open. First close your eyes, then breathe deeply in and out through your nose. Slowly open your eyes and gaze at the flame.

To make you fully equipped for effective psychic action, meditation should become a completely normal activity in your life—as routine as brushing your teeth. However, forcing yourself to do it can be counter-productive—two minutes of complete connection to inner silence is far better than sitting still for 20 minutes without reaching the still voice within. It is quality not quantity that counts.

Mystics believe that meditation is the path to self-enlightenment. Eastern traditions refer to the need to calm the "monkey mind"—the busy, active level of thinking. Deep meditation gives you the power to do this; it enables you to concentrate your thoughts, rather than chasing after every passing notion. Thinking with this level of clarity is the essential ingredient of self-mastery—it is true freedom.

TM

In the 1960s the Maharishi Mahesh Yogi popularized Transcendental Meditation (TM), which uses a sound or mantra to help with focusing during meditation. This might be a single word such as "love," "peace" or "beauty" or the ancient sound "om" (said to be the original sound from which the universe was created); the primary factor is that it resonates both mentally and emotionally. Transcendental Meditation has attracted many followers since, and is still a widely used technique.

AIDS TO MEDITATION
The visual stimulus of a simple object such as a leaf, shell, candle, flower, or pebble can help to concentrate your mind during meditation. So, too, can a pleasing fragrance such as incense, or a mandala as shown opposite. Always use what works for you—these are just a few suggestions.

Tuning in to Your Chakras

A psychic perceives centers of spinning energy, sometimes seen as radiant colors, at seven points along your spinal column. These are chakras, key locations on a pathway of energy flowing from head to toe. This "pranic" energy derives from the highest planes of consciousness, and acts in different ways at each chakra. When your chakras are functioning properly, they allow etheric energy to flow through freely, balancing you in mind, body, and spirit and giving you complete harmony.

The chakra centers are an important part of the picture a psychic sees when viewing your aura; they act as focal points for a psychic "scan." A gifted psychic can assess your entire physical, emotional, and mental state by "reading" your chakras and aura. As described opposite, each chakra radiates the energy of its color; starting from the top of the body, these are violet, indigo, blue, green, yellow, orange, and red. They indicate how you interact with the world and experience yourself (see page 44).

THE CHAKRAS
Positioned at seven centers on your body, your chakras (right) are associated with the lotus, regarded as a sacred flower in India. The unfolding petals correspond to the opening up of a chakra. Each chakra is depicted with a number of petals, starting with the four petals of the base center, and moving upward to the crown, which is called the thousand or many-petalled lotus. The functions of the chakras are described on the opposite page.

The Crown Center *Sahasrara*
Key energy: "I know."
Set at the top of the head, this chakra represents pure thought. It connects you with infinite consciousness, the highest energy in the universe. By expanding the crown, you can tap into the deepest sources of spiritual wisdom.

The Brow Center *Ajna*
Key energy: "I see."
This chakra is in the middle of the forehead and acts as the window of the "third eye." Opening this center gives you vision beyond ordinary sight. It enhances your clairvoyance, enabling you to see past, present, and future.

The Heart Center *Anahata*
Key energy: "I love."
Situated at the center of your body, this chakra acts as the bridge between the physical and spiritual worlds. Activating it increases your power of love, compassion, and empathy with others.

The Throat Center
Visuddha
Key energy: "I speak up."
Positioned in the throat, this center of communication connects with hearing and speech. Activating it inspires you to speak and listen in the spirit of truth. It also promotes spiritual communication and improves psychic hearing ability, or clairaudience.

The Solar Plexus Center *Manipura*
Key energy: "I can."
Based in the stomach area, this chakra represents vitality and will. Opening it puts you in touch with your personal power, and transforms your hopes and aspirations into real possibilities.

The Sacral Center *Svadhisthana*
Key energy: "I feel/want."
The rocket-like energy of this center is generated from its site at the lower abdomen, between the navel and genitals. Opening it releases your innate creativity and fertility. It propels you into action and fuels your emotions and sexuality.

The Base Center *Muladhara*
Key energy: "I have."
This chakra is located at the base of the spine. It is always open, linking you to the earth and sheer physical survival. Energizing it grounds you in a healthy desire for the basics of life—food, warmth, and shelter.

Your overall sense of well-being depends on the unimpeded flow of etheric energy through your chakras (see preceding pages). If one of these centers is blocked, you may not feel entirely at ease with yourself. This is why it's important to keep this energy moving freely. The breathing exercise (page 31) is an excellent balancing routine that you can do regularly, and you can use the visualization (below) to check for any problems in your chakras.

If you feel that a specific center needs freeing up, there are simple ways to do this. For instance, to invigorate your base center, try energetic dancing, jumping up and down, stamping your feet, jogging, and kicking out. Anything that gets your hips moving is good for the sacral center, including pelvic rocking movements. Moving your belly frees up the solar plexus—have fun with a hula-hoop or enjoy a session of belly dancing. To stimulate your heart center, you need to expand your chest—swimming is effective, also stretching your arms. Ease the throat center with gentle neck rolls and open your brow center by rolling your eyes in all directions, stretching them as far as they can go. Finally, to energize your crown center, stand on your head for a few minutes. By keeping all your chakras open, you'll gain a deeper sense of self.

An experimental journey

There are no right or wrong answers in this exercise. But it will help to free up your mind and identify symbols that you may need in psychic work. It also gives access to your unconscious and any underlying imbalances.

Focus your mind onto each of your chakras, and let yourself be drawn intuitively toward one of them. Now visualize a door in front of you that is the signature color of that chakra. See yourself opening this door, then entering the room beyond. Now consider these questions:

- ❏ What does the room look like?
- ❏ What is on the walls?
- ❏ What furniture is in the room?
- ❏ Is there a closet or drawers? If so, what is inside them?
- ❏ Is there a picture on the wall? If so, describe it.
- ❏ How does the room feel generally?
- ❏ Is anyone else in the room? If so, what is he or she communicating to you?
- ❏ How reluctant are you to leave the room?

Assessment

The way you feel about this room relates to the energy of the chakra you chose. So, if you walk into the yellow room of the solar plexus, you are dealing with your sense of power or helplessness. If you see colors that are strong, vibrant and clear, that's fine; but if they are dark or muddy, you have problems to resolve. Furniture represents encumbrances and anything found inside drawers or closets relates to what you need to discard. Also, any picture on the walls is an image of yourself. Psychically, the healthiest state for the room is to be completely empty. If your room is muddled and cluttered, you have a lot of unfinished business connected with the area of yourself that you are exploring here.

BALANCING YOUR CHAKRAS BY BREATHING IN COLOR ENERGY

1 *Focus on your breath as described on page 23, then shift your attention to your base chakra. As you breathe, visualize powerful red energy from the earth's core glowing inside this chakra.*

2 *Now move up to the sacral center; breathe quietly, and see bright orange flames of fire burning in the chakra.*

3 *Next, breathe bright yellow sunlight into the solar plexus, warming you and filling you with comfort.*

4 *Now absorb the vibrant green of fresh grass into your heart chakra.*

5 *Then focus on the throat: breathe in the pure blue of a summer sky.*

6 *Breathe the radiant indigo of the evening sky into your brow center. A crystal clear energy cuts through and gives you a higher vision.*

7 *Now breathe violet light into your crown center, letting in the pure light of divine consciousness. Acknowledge yourself as a spiritual entity.*

8 *Draw pure light down into each center in a column of pure energy, keeping the flow of your breathing.*

9 *Focus into your heart center and feel the balance and harmony throughout your centers. Now visualize a circle of golden light around yourself. Finally, concentrate on your feet, and feel a strong root of energy linking them to the earth.*

Use the color pages 122–37 to aid your meditation.

Understanding Your Will

An experienced psychic knows that it is possible to exert one's will by energetically focusing his or her thoughts (thoughts and emotions are forms of energy and energy follows thought). Directed thought is a powerful tool in spiritual and healing work, but always remember to use it responsibly. When you send out thought energy, you must know and mean *precisely* what you're implementing.

Examine every aspect before following through. And never activate a thought or action against someone's wishes, no matter how loving your intent. You may assume that you're innocent of imposing your will on others, but check the questions opposite, then think about the kinds of will described below. You'll realize that subtle forms such as karmic and divine will are just as important as the more direct styles.

The four types of will

Can you recognize your personal style of implementing your will? Do you go with the flow, or leave nothing to chance? Each has a valuable part to play.

Strong will
You use this will directly, compelling yourself or others to do your bidding. If this results in fine achievements, it is a positive force. But bullying or ignoring other people's needs is harmful.

Skillful will
This wily approach gets you what you want by indirect means. You may manipulate others by open charm or hidden subterfuge. Fox-like, clever, you achieve your ends by stealth.

Karmic will
This is the subtle will of cause and effect—"what goes around, comes around." Your past actions can react on the present with inevitable force, making you reap what you've sown.

Divine will
This is all-powerful, and goes beyond your personal will to the universal level, connecting you with your higher or spiritual self. It unifies heavenly and personal will.

Where there's a will...
Any psychic action needs careful thought; this means adopting the right mental attitude to each situation. If you're a forceful person, you may be tempted to solve a problem using your Strong will. But this could be a mistake—Karmic will may be at work, for example. Or it may be better to employ the indirect Skillful will. Keep an open mind and let your intuition decide what response is needed. Then adapt your will to act in an appropriate manner.

What kind of will do you have?

Read the questions below and check *only* those to which you have an affirmative response.

❏ 1 Do you often wonder why people are negative toward you?

❏ 2 Are you able to fulfil your ambitions effectively?

❏ 3 If you want something, do you take time to work out how to achieve it?

❏ 4 Do you take other people into account when you make decisions?

❏ 5 When you make decisions, do you consider what is for the highest good irrespective of what you yourself feel?

❏ 6 If you want something, do you persist until you get it?

❏ 7 Are you able to accept difficult situations as part of a greater plan?

❏ 8 Are you able to go with the flow of events and find some learning experience in everything that happens?

❏ 9 Are you able to get other people to do what you want without them realizing it?

❏ 10 Do you consider very carefully your actions as ones that are intuitively right?

❏ 11 Do you ever try to persuade people to do something they are unsure of?

❏ 12 Can you keep your mind centered on a question without being distracted?

Assessment

Look at your total of "yes" answers. Do all, or most of them, fit into one of the groups of numbers below? If so, this will give you a good idea of what kind of will you have.

If you had an equal distribution of yes answers, you're well-balanced and exert your will flexibly and positively.

2 6 11
You often implement a STRONG will

Make sure this is not at the expense of others: remember that what you give out will always return. Exertion of your will over others is a form of psychic attack.

3 9 12
Yours is a SKILLFUL will

You use skill to achieve what you want. Be careful that it is not used to manipulate others against their own will, as ultimately no good will come from it.

1 4 10
You're aware of KARMIC will

You're a very thoughtful person and respect the natural laws of cause and effect. Therefore, you're more likely to receive positive thoughts and actions from others.

5 7 8
You trust in DIVINE will

You're insightful and altruistic. You are the person most likely to find happiness and contentment, as you are able to perceive an overview to life and a greater meaning in everything.

Using Positive Thought

Directed thought is the keynote to psychic activity—and each thought has an immensely powerful energy. Knowing this, you can implement concentrated mental force to free yourself from any negative thought patterns. In doing so, you will enhance your self-confidence, deepen your psychic powers, and enjoy a much more productive life.

At first, simply listen to yourself. Do you often start a sentence with a phrase like "I'm afraid," or "I'm sorry?" Have you ever heard yourself saying "Knowing my luck!" If you analyze the thought messages that are being sent out with these words, you'll know exactly why you never *do* have any luck. Shifting old patterns can be hard work. But don't give up; you'll be rewarded.

If you "bad-mouth" someone, that particular energy will come back to you. Everyone has something unique to offer, so use your psychic insight to identify each person's good qualities.

Don't be drawn into negative conversations. If, for instance, a friend regularly becomes involved in disastrous relationships, be sympathetic; then ask the friend what he or she can learn from that pattern to prevent the same thing happening in the future.

While positive thought has many benefits, it can't be used as a panacea for all ills. It should never be a way of hiding or denying pain. If you do have a problem, confront it, then use effective affirmations to change any damaging, fixed patterns of behavior.

The golden rules

Get yourself into a relaxed, meditative state (see page 23), and ask for an inspirational statement that you can affirm each day to promote your well-being. Use the following guidelines to point the way:

Keep it simple.

Be inventive.

Convert it into a memorable rhyme or catchphrase—no more than four lines.

Say your affirmation out loud at least three times a day, for at least 28 days.

Always refer to the first person in your affirmation—say "I" or "Me."

AFFIRMATIONS

Health	*"My body is the temple of my soul and looks after me perfectly."*
Courage	*"I am one with the universe and safe at all times."*
Employment	*"Perfect work for perfect pay is coming my way."*
Love	*"I love the world and it loves me."*
Success	*"Abundance and success now come to me in endless ways."*
Happiness	*"I am balanced, joyful, happy and radiant and detached from any fear."*
Prosperity	*"The universe is an endless source which pours wealth upon me."*

ONWARD AND UPWARD

Once you've learned to harness the power of positive thought, you'll find yourself on the stairway to success. Use this extraordinary technique to improve every aspect of your life, to help you get a better job, to improve your talents, or to bring you radiant good health.

Exerting Mind over Matter

You may have used positive thought to change your emotions and behavior (see preceding pages), but it is a much greater challenge to accept that you can use the same energy to affect objects. This ability is known as psychokinesis or PK. As yet, there is no final answer as to why some people can influence the "heads or tails" fall of coins, stop clocks, or stop and start computers. But researchers have identified a specific pattern in the brain waves of people while they are implementing PK. These findings may be the key to this ability—and you, too, can develop the skill. It can give you that vital "edge" over events, and improve your luck on bets with cards or dice. Try the experiments featured on the page opposite and overleaf—they will all help to enhance your psychokinetic aptitude.

Once you've acquired the knack of applying PK energy, you can use it in lots of ways. For instance, during a game of pool or golf, your ball may be poised on the edge of the hole or the pocket. When this happens, try "willing" your ball to drop into place—you'll be amazed how often you will succeed in doing this. Using the same, concentrated thought energy, you may also find that you'll be able to stop or start clocks and computers.

ACTIVATING THOUGHT ENERGY

If you can acquire the knack, this exercise provides direct feedback to boost your PK ability. Suspend your rational self, believe it is possible and "know" you can do it.

1 *Put a candle in a holder, light it, then place it on a table in a quiet, dimly lit room. The air in the room should be as still as possible.*

2 *Sit at the table at least 18 inches in front of the candle. Get yourself completely relaxed (see page 23). Look directly into the heart of the flame, and keep gazing steadily until you feel completely attuned to its movement, rhythm, and energy.*

3 *When you're ready, shift your gaze to a spot about 1 inch above the flame. Focus there in a relaxed manner until you feel the flame "pulling" upward.*

4 *As soon as this happens, direct a sudden charge of concentrated energy into the flame; doing this boosts its upward movement, raising its level.*

5 *Hold the flame there as long as you can, then relax your gaze and allow the flame to drop to its original level.*

BEATING THE ODDS

When you throw a playing card into the air, the odds are 50–50 that it will land face down or up. Can you use your mind to improve the average outcome?

1 *Make yourself completely relaxed (see page 23) and decide in advance whether you want the card to land face down or up.*

2 *Toss a card into the air, and, as it moves, actively "will" it to fall the way you want. Do this 100 times and mark down each result.*

3 *Make a control group of another 100 throws by not trying to target the outcome. Mark down the results—they should be close to the normal 50–50 average distribution.*

4 *Add up your "targeted" score. If you've achieved something like 65 correct "hits," you're showing positive PK ability.*

If you got positive results from basic psychokinetic exercises such as raising a candle flame and making clocks stop (see preceding pages), you'll have experienced the satisfaction of seeing your own thought power at work. But there are even more ways to apply focused mental energy; for example, you may have heard of people who can move objects just by concentrating on them. This is possible, but it's not easy to get results on your own.

The best way to succeed in moving things with applied mental energy is to work with others. If you belong to a psychic development group, you'll already be accustomed to synchronizing your energies. But has your group tried applying its combined thought force to moving inanimate items? Small groups meeting regularly on a relaxed, informal basis have obtained the best results. It's been shown that these PK experimental sessions are a challenging way to sharpen psychic teamwork skills.

If you're not a member of a psychic group, you could simply ask some friends to join you in the exercise described below. This can be risky, however: even people you know very well might be tempted to "help" a successful outcome to occur, so stay alert.

USING GROUP FORCE

The combined energies of a psychic group can be harnessed to make objects move. Try it and see.

1 *Choose an enclosed unit, preferably made of glass. A glass box with a fitted lid is ideal so you can watch, but not touch, any object inside.*

2 *Place the item you wish to move at the bottom of the container. Use things like sugar or coffee grounds at first and try moving small, solid objects, such as a needle, later. Put the box on a table in full view of the whole group.*

3 *Seat the group around the table. Everyone should now get into a lightly relaxed, meditative state—remember, too much concentration can be counter-productive.*

4 *You can either ask a trusted spirit entity for help, or give a name to the active thought energy of of the group. You could call it "the agency" for instance.*

5 *The group should now quietly concentrate on linking with a spirit or "agency" and ask it to help them move the object in the box.*

6 *If materials such as coffee granules or sugar are being used, the spirit or "agency" can be asked to leave a trail, pattern, or a message. Whatever result the group requires, each person should powerfully visualize this.*

7 *Focus the group's concentration in short bursts—twenty minutes at most. Don't continue this exercise if anyone in the group becomes frightened or senses a sinister energy.*

Sharpen Your Psychic Vision

Have you sometimes noticed an odd shadow out of the corner of your eye, seen a colored mist around a person or animal, or glimpsed pinpoints of floating light? These are examples of psychic sight—the ability to see energies that are normally invisible to the naked eye. This is an extremely useful skill; it not only adds an extra dimension to your daily awareness of the world about you, it also enables you to focus on someone's aura (see page 42), and enhances clairvoyance (see page 90). You can develop your psychic vision by doing the exercises shown below and on the opposite page. They give you the flexibility to switch your visual focus automatically.

A PERCEPTION-SHIFTING EXERCISE

Not all pictures are what they seem to be at first glance. What do you see when you look at the picture, shown right. A well-known person or a myriad of tiny images with a larger one in the center? Now try holding the page much further away from you and tilting it slightly. What do you see now?

THIRD-EYE VISION

Ancient Egyptian hieroglyphs often depict the image of the "third eye," an invisible center of psychic perception located behind the pineal gland in the head. Third-eye vision is a magical art used by priests, priestesses, and seers, and takes years, even lifetimes, to mature. It is an immensely powerful tool—giving a complete overview of life, as if you were looking down at events on the ground from an aircraft.

ENHANCING PSYCHIC FOCUS

Improving your abilities to work with observable phenomena will help you see what others may not.

1 *Get yourself thoroughly relaxed (see page 23), and extend your arms out fully in front of your body. Hold your two forefingers upright—about 6 inches apart is fine.*

2 *Concentrate on the space between your fingers, keeping a steady gaze for a few moments.*

3 *Next, gently draw the fingers together until they merge into one. Be aware of how your focus moves to the position of this image. It could be to*

the right or to the left, depending upon which finger receives the greater part of your attention.

4 *Do this repeatedly until you can visualize a third finger without the help of the other two.*

5 *The position of this third finger is where you should look when reading an aura (see page 42) or doing a psychic "scan." Use a relaxed half-focused gaze.*

Looking at the Aura

All living things have a complex electrical field or "aura" surrounding them. Some people are born with the ability to see this with the naked eye, and describe luminous, shimmering bands of rainbow color radiating from, and encircling, the body. There are various theories about the source of this radiant energy: it is widely believed to emanate from the highest plane of consciousness, entering and leaving your body through your chakras (see page 28). You also can think of an aura as a powerful electromagnetic field, equipping you with superb sensitivity to external influences, and sending your own energy vibrations into the world.

Recent studies using blindfold tests have shown that people can "sense" when someone is staring at them intently, even if they can't see the person doing it. Researchers believe that this information is picked up within the aura.

The human aura is a complete physical, emotional, mental, and spiritual "map" of a person's life and character. It reveals patterns of thought, as well as the ebb and flow of physical and emotional energy, and will show any areas that need healing or energizing. Before you set out to explore the map of someone else's aura, get to know your own first, using the techniques described opposite.

IMAGING THE AURA

The Soviet husband and wife team Semyon and Valentina Kirlian were the first to capture a photographic image of the aura. Technology has progressed rapidly since—the British radiologist Dr Walter Kilner devised special "screens" to view the aura, and, as a result, many psychics have learned how to diagnose and heal illnesses through the aura. You can obtain a color photograph of your aura at psychic conventions. Kirlian photography is still widely used. A famous example is the Kirlian image of a leaf with half of its area removed. The leaf appears whole in the photograph—the energy radiating from it is not affected.

DISCOVERING YOUR OWN AURA

Use this technique to explore the energy field around your body.

1 *Work in a dimly lit room. Sit in front of a clear area of wall. Relax (see page 23).*

2 *Stretch your arms out in front of you, one hand facing down, the other up.*

3 *Quickly squeeze your hands together. After one or two minutes, reverse hands, and keep squeezing until you feel them pulling.*

4 *Drop your hands down by your sides. Then, slowly raise them with the palms facing. Bring your hands together very slowly until you sense a*

point of resistance. Feel your hands attracting each other like magnets, but don't let your palms touch.

5 *Lightly half-focus your gaze (see page 41) at the area around your hands. You may see a halo of light around them—even a color. Note this, and feel the energy built up between your hands. You may get a pulsing, tingling feeling—that is your aura.*

AURA CHECK

Your aura reacts to mood, people, and places. You can take a quick look at its main color at any time, using this method.

1 *It's difficult to see your own aura in its entirety, but you can easily check its current predominant color.*

2 *Focus closely on the rainbow illustrated here, then gaze at your face in a mirror, backlit with a soft, dim light. Close your eyes, and visualize the rainbow over your head.*

3 *Open your eyes quickly, and look at the halo of color(s) above your head. This is your key aura color at present.*

4 *Use the color chart on the next pages to interpret the color or colors you see. And when you check your aura another time, note how the colors have changed.*

Most of us are aware of color in auras, even though this may be a subliminal insight. Your unconscious vision is reflected in the most casual remarks—for example, you may note that someone is in a "black mood," "browned off," "red with anger," "green with envy," "in the pink," or "feeling blue." These intuitive comments are your response to the predominant color radiating from someone's aura at any one time—a rapid psychic snapshot. However, it requires a finely tuned sensitivity to decipher each different shade in the rainbow of the aura.

The constant play of color reflects changing thoughts, impulses, and emotions, and it is deeply fascinating to explore the meaning of each shade (see right). Try not to be obsessed with every tiny detail, however—it's equally important to note how the colors make you feel in reaction to the emotional energy they project. What is your response to a particular color? Is it flowing easily? Or is it sharp and spiky? Most important, is it strong and pure? Dirty, patchy areas are not good news.

Always remember that the colors of your aura are directly related to your chakras, and the best way to get and keep a balanced, healthy, aura is to breathe color into each chakra center, as shown on page 31.

Red

Vibrantly active, red reveals physical energy or anger. A deep crimson may mean a high sex drive while scarlet denotes ego. A pure, bright red can restore depleted physical energy.

Pink

Rose pink is a sign of unselfish love and sensitivity. This is the color of a practicing healer, or may indicate that spiritual healing is currently being implemented.

Green

A clear, fresh green shows balance and growth; a pastel shade, spirituality. Dark green indicates envy and selfishness. Muddy, olive green denotes greed, deceit or depression.

Blue

This can be a deeply healing color, and indicates an independent spirit. Dark blue areas in the aura show stubbornness or dogmatism — but a deep navy blue is highly protective.

Orange
Bright orange is a sign of healthy sexuality. Muddy shades mean self-indulgence. Reddish orange suggests slyness. If it is "flaming" off the body, it denotes sex running riot.

Yellow
Clear, bright yellow signifies intellect, warmth and compassion. A muddy or dark shade denotes a fearful, resentful, lazy person who thinks the world owes him or her something.

Gold
This truly spiritual color is rarely seen in the aura—it is the sign of saints or godly beings, as depicted in haloes. Used in healing, gold is an excellent overall aid and protection.

Silver
When surrounded by this color, the person has erratic mental energy. He or she lives a life of illusion, and may be mentally ill. Silver can also be protective—visualize it around your car.

Indigo/Violet
Indigo is the timeless color signature of the priest or priestess, and is emanated by the seeker of truth. A pure violet signifies an intensely spiritual person.

Gray/Black
A band of black or gray over the head shows that a person suffers depressed thoughts. Situated on the solar plexus and lower body, they indicate negative emotions.

Brown
This points to a materialistic person with good business acumen and organizational skills. A muddy brown indicates the need to get what he or she wants immediately.

White
Like gold, this is not a color that is often seen within the human aura. It always indicates a highly evolved, divinely spiritual being—such as a saint or holy mystic.

Making a complete summary of everything you see within the aura is a subtle art. You'll certainly need to have a clear idea of its structure, and where the different colors are located. This is a vital key to understanding the significance of all the shades of color that you see there.

To focus your thoughts, look at the illustration on the facing page. It shows that the human aura is made up of seven layers that are powered by the chakras (see page 28). These subtle layers radiate outward in bands of color surrounding the body. The quality of these colors are the major clues to what is happening on each level—when they are bright and pure, that is a good sign; but muddy, dirty, clashing, or unharmonious shades indicate problem areas.

If you learn to view the aura clearly, you'll have a privileged insight. You may see great contrasts and extremes of strength and vulnerability. You'll also gain deep knowledge of someone's inner character, feelings, thoughts, and psychic gifts.

If you enjoy drawing, try making colored sketches of the aura—this sharpens your observation, and improves your accuracy. If you want to do healing or energizing work on the aura you can consult your sketches to double-check the areas where you found problems.

MAKING AN AURA PORTRAIT

Character, thoughts, feelings, pain, happiness, strength, weakness—they're all visible in the aura.

1 *Assemble some sheets of cream paper and a box of colored crayons. Ask a friend to sit in front of a white or light-colored wall, then get relaxed (see page 23).*

2 *Lightly gaze at the area around the edges of your friend's body. Your eyes should be half-focused (see page 41) onto the wall behind him or her.*

3 *Wait until you can see (or sense) the outlines of your friend's energy field. When you see colors, ask your friend to shift position: the colors should move at the same time.*

4 *Now draw the aura. Keep looking and checking; note exactly where the colors are situated, and indicate if they are light or dark. Use the color references on the preceding pages as a guide to interpreting the colors, but, in the final analysis, always trust your own intuition.*

Each chakra is associated with a particular energy (see page 28) and each energy type manifests itself as a color.

Red *is the color of the base, or lowest chakra;*

Orange *the color of the sacral chakra;*

Yellow *the color of the solar plexus chakra;*

Green *that of the heart chakra;*

Blue *of the throat chakra;*

Indigo *of the brow chakra and*

Violet *that of the crown chakra.*

A lot can be learned by studying the intensity, clarity and amount of each color and relating this back to the energy's "meaning."

EXTRA-SENSORY PERCEPTION

2

Could You be a Mind Reader?

Have you known what someone was going to say seconds before he or she verbalized it? If so, you've experienced a form of telepathy—the ability to read minds. This psychic gift is immensely useful; it gives you razor-sharp sensitivity and makes you aware of what others are really thinking. You'll be able to interpret their hidden needs with uncanny accuracy. This is useful in all situations—whether you're trying to work out what your boss really wants from you, or discovering why your friend has suddenly become very reserved.

Telepathic ability has been widely studied by ESP researchers because the data from controlled "mind reading" experiments can be measured against statistical probability. You can improve your own telepathic skills by using well-proven techniques, such as sending and receiving simple images (see below) and by following the information set out on the following pages.

The classic method for testing mind-reading was devised by psychic researcher Karl Zener. He created a series of five cards with simple symbols—a circle, a square, a cross, a star, and a set of wavy lines. They have become major tools in psychic research. You can buy these, but it's easy to create your own deck—get 25 plain postcards and make five cards of each symbol. Draw the symbols clearly, but make sure they are not visible through the card.

ZENER TELEPATHY TEST

1 *Working with a friend, decide which of you is to be the "sender" and which the "receiver" of the images, then sit in separate rooms. Both need to be familiar with the images.*

2 *The sender shuffles the 25 cards, then, concentrating on one image for three minutes at a time, mentally "beams" the image to the receiver. The receiver should make a note of the picture he or she "sees"—generally what appears first. A bell, handclap or mobile phone can be used to signal the start of a new "transmission."*

3 *Once the sequence of 25 cards has been tested, check the results and record the scores. There is a 20–25% chance of guessing the correct answer. Consistently correct scores of over 25% indicate a high telepathic ability.*

4 *A quick and easy test can be done by using the grid of Zener images shown on the opposite page. Decide in which direction you'll work—sideways across or top down—then mentally send the images in sequence, spending three minutes concentrating on each. The receiver takes notes as before. How many of the received images were correct?*

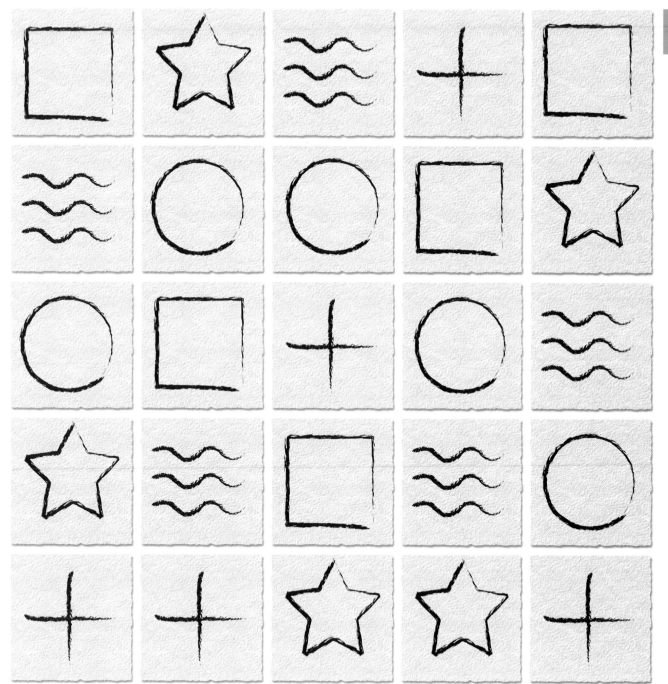

The next stage in improving your telepathy skills is to use completely random images that the "receiver" has not seen previously. This is more difficult than working with Zener cards (see preceding pages), as their simple, graphic images are known to both the sender and the receiver.

It will certainly be helpful if you are mentally and emotionally close to the person with whom you are collaborating. And if it's someone with whom you've already experienced "flashes" of telepathic contact, so much the better. This often happens with people who are related—for instance, the mental bond between twins can be extraordinary.

The exercise and guidelines shown here can help you to achieve an even more advanced psychic state of telepathic sending and receiving. Be open to every sign and impression that you receive, and use your imagination to sense your way through to the image.

RECEIVING UNSEEN IMAGES

Ask a trusted friend to beam you a picture that you've never seen before.

1 *Your friend should choose a random image to send—it could be a postcard or a picture from a book, for example. At first, it is best to use simple, graphic images such as an animal, a tree, or a building.*

2 *At a mutually agreed time, your friend concentrates on the picture and actively "beams" it to you.*

3 *Prepare yourself to receive the incoming picture by getting completely relaxed—use the breathing exercise on page 23.*

4 *Let any sensations and impressions come into your mind. As they arrive, simply register them without questioning, and make a mental note of any image you see.*

5 *When you're ready, return to your normal state of consciousness. While the pictures are fresh in your mind either draw the images you saw, or write detailed notes so that you can check the results with your friend.*

Telepathy boosters

Avoid second-guessing what the image might be.

Allow your mind to be as free-ranging as possible.

Don't try to analyze how the choice may have been made by the sender.

As soon as images start coming through, don't dismiss them as ideas from your own mind.

Keep a particular lookout for images and thoughts that seem to come from nowhere—those that just suddenly appear.

When you make notes, describe what you saw in as much detail as you can, but do not invent or exaggerate anything.

Don't be despondent if you didn't receive any images, or if they were inaccurate. Keep trying, you'll eventually get a hit—perhaps much sooner than you imagine.

Alternate between being the sender and the receiver.

GUIDING YOUR PERCEPTION

An image may be of a person, thing, place, or situation. As a picture forms in your mind, register its main characteristics and zero in on these.

Are you sensing an outdoor scene?

If so, what is it like? Are you looking up into the sky? Seeing a mountain, a beach, a stretch of ocean—or is it part of a garden? What is the key element in the view? Is it a bird, an aircraft, a balloon, a sculpture? Can you see a large tree? A sail boat? Or a garden seat?

Does the image you're getting suggest a person?

If so, are you sensing a man or a woman? An adult or a child? Is the person doing something? Is he or she sitting or standing? Holding something? Playing a game? Is the person dressed in any special clothes? Or using any tools or equipment?

Do you feel you are looking at a particular item or thing?

Are you in an office or part of a hospital? Or a room in a home? Can you pick out the central focus of the scene? Is it an item or furniture such as a table, chair, fireplace, or couch, or some other object such as a bowl of fruit, a vase of flowers, a framed photograph, or a birthday cake?

Can You See a Place You've Never Been?

During the dark days of the Cold War, rumors circulated about a new spying technique. Psychic expertise was being used to develop the ability to "see" things from a distance. American surveillance experts trained personnel in the art of remote viewing. This is the ability to tune into a place anywhere on the planet and see what is there —it should be possible to look into any room across the world and take in what is happening inside. Remote viewing also can be used to see a person or object, which is some distance away. Remote viewing works similarly to mental telepathy (see page 52) except that information is not transmitted by another but rather, people pick up information without it being "sent."

A Rare Gift

Remote viewing's most exciting aspect is that it literally opens up your world, as you can travel far and wide without leaving home. The psychic Ingo Swann was once given a latitude and longitude position over the telephone by someone he had never met. Immediately he identified a rocky island—there were some buildings there, including an orange structure. He described the coastline and other details. These geographical coordinates marked the island of Kerguelen, where the French had a research base studying the upper atmosphere. Swann had no prior knowledge of this, yet his description was eerily accurate.

As for its practical applications, it would be a great help to those in the creative professions. Novelists and writers could use it to give realistic descriptions of well-known places in their work. Artists, too, could use it to make paintings, backdrops, and stage sets of places they themselves are too busy to travel to. On a more every day basis, you're more likely to use it to keep benign track of your loved ones. It's a great way to "accompany" relatives and friends who are away from home. Parents of teenagers, especially, might welcome being kept "informed" of the whereabouts of their youngsters. But always remember to respect an individual's privacy—a loving check is acceptable, obsessive snooping is not.

Testing Proficiency

Professionally, people known to have the gift of remote viewing are often asked to help police find missing persons or remains and to assist with criminal investigations. They can be helpful, for example, in locating the wreckage of aircraft that crash in mountainous or thickly forested places.

Scientists test for remote viewing abilities by having an outsider pick one photograph from many hundreds. This photograph is subsequently hidden; no person involved in the experiment sees it. The person being assessed is then asked to describe the photograph's contents. An independent panel then assesses the correctness of the description. You can try out your abilities using the exercise opposite.

EXPERIENCING REMOTE VIEWING

For your first efforts, choose a place to "visit" that you've never seen before, but is known to a trusted friend. It could be his or her previous home or workplace, or somewhere that he or she has visited, for example.

1 *Get completely relaxed and close your eyes so you achieve a meditative state. Focus on your breathing, then imaginatively travel to your destination, and slowly enter the site.*

2 *Look around carefully; what do you see? Describe to your friend the colors, textures, furniture, walls, doors, ceilings, pets, people—and take note of anything unusual—any odd detail that catches your attention.*

3 *Once you're satisfied that you've seen enough, take yourself back to your familiar body.*

4 *Check with your friend that you got the details right. Or, if he or she isn't there with you, make sure you record some notes to share with him or her later.*

What Can an Object Tell You?

If you remember ever saying something like "this ring always makes me feel strange when I wear it" or "I don't like the feel of this garment," you may have experienced a form of psychometry. This is the art of sensing energies from inanimate objects. Any object—something small, such as a piece of jewelry or larger, such an item of furniture—can be "read." All objects have their own, unique energy fields and these fields pick up vibrations from the people and places with which they are associated. Even if an object has been in someone's possession for a very short time, it will have absorbed into its energy field that person's particular vibration.

One obvious use for such a gift would be to determine the rightful owner of a found object. It also would be beneficial for healers of all types as clients often withhold information that is germane to their situations or conditions. Reading someone's possession is one way of gaining knowledge without being intrusive.

But as with many psychic abilities, what one gets from such a gift may not be immediately apparent to all—except as a source of wonder. Most psychics believe that information communicated through a sixth sense provides yet another layer through which the world and everything in it can be comprehended. Knowledge is power after all.

READING AN OBJECT'S ENERGIES

Ask the person for whom you are doing a reading to let you hold something belonging to him or her. A ring or watch that has been worn for a long time is a good choice.

1 *Hold the item lightly in your hands and direct your thoughts (and therefore your energy) onto the object. It may help you to concentrate if you close your eyes.*

2 *Visualize yourself sending an arrow of thought to link with the object. Then immediately relax and allow impressions to float into your mind. In doing this, the energy you are using is both active and receptive. You need both kinds when doing psychic work.*

3 *Note exactly what you are receiving, whether it is an image, sensation, thought, or any kind of impression. Discount nothing; even the faintest feeling may be an indication. On the other hand, psychometry can be very physical and you may experience quite distinct sensations such as an object turning hot or cold.*

4 *Try not to be deterred by the notion that these thoughts and impressions are "just in the mind." Simply accept*

that all information has to travel through your mind. You may receive familiar images, but this does not mean they are unimportant.

5 *Tell the person exactly what you see; don't omit or embellish anything. Avoid projecting your judgments and experiences onto what you are seeing.*

Insider info PSYCHOMETRY

The most immediate perceptions *are images of what the owner of the object you are reading has been thinking, feeling, and doing over the last 24–48 hours.*

Strongly-held thoughts *and feelings or emotionally charged actions will persist in an object's vibrations for years. Those that are fleeting, however, produce similar short-lived energies.*

How much you can tell about past owners *depends on the object's history. If you tune into an object inherited by a daughter whose mother died 20 years previously, you may not receive much information about her mother. However, if the daughter is still very affected by her mother's death, you may receive more of a picture of the original owner.*

Can You Sense Things that Others Can't?

Some people have an exceptional gift for sensing things that are out of the range of ordinary perception. This is known as clairsentience, a form of intuition that deals with infinitely fragile, subtle energies, which are accessed in seemingly inexplicable ways. One way of developing a heightened sensitivity is by connecting with the benign energy of living plants (see below). This can imbue you with a vibrant sense of well-being. Positive energy then will emanate back from you to the plant, creating a dynamic, beneficial cycle. By establishing an active psychic relationship with nature, your senses will become alive to everything around you and you will acquire information beyond others' knowing.

GETTING IN TOUCH WITH NATURE

All flowers, plants, and trees generate beneficial energy, which can be comprehended as their "guardian spirits." To tune into this positive force, visit a favorite outdoor spot and let yourself be drawn to a particular tree, plant, or flower.

1 *Sit under or close by your chosen plant so you move inside its aura.*

2 *Once you're in a serene, meditative state, spend some time connecting to your breath (see page 23); then, when you are centered, focus your breath into your heart center.*

3 *Literally open your heart and wait. Nature energies are on a different frequency to yours, so, if you have never tried this before, you may need plenty of time to tune yourself in.*

4 *Receive the energy from the plant, and quietly ask its guardian spirit to communicate with you.*

5 *Your sense of smell is a good route into the plant's energy, so be aware of the scents surrounding you. If you make a good link, you may sense the breath of the spirit. It feels as if you are being stroked by butterfly wings.*

6 *Be open to any impressions you receive, and cherish this privileged contact with nature.*

UNDERSTANDING THE LANGUAGE OF FLOWERS

Although connecting with the "spirit" of a flower may provide you with insights that surpass any ordinary knowing, you also can learn a great deal about a person from looking at the color, shape, and aspect of his or her favorite flower.

Primary or pastel? *The shade of the bloom can tell you a lot about the person. Bright yellow flowers, for example, suit someone with a keen intellect, while red flowers are associated with fiery natures.*

Flower away from or close to its leaves? *If the flower stands apart from other parts of the plant, this indicates independence and/or ambition. Proximity signals dependence.*

Single or multiple blooms? *If the former, the person may be a bit of a loner. Lots of blooms and leaves on the stem points to someone sociable who loves having people around.*

Straight, twisted, long, or short stems? *Stems show a person's path in life. Are they straight or twisty, long or short? The lower section describes the past or youth, the middle the present or adulthood, the top the future or old age.*

Strong and healthy flower? *If so, this should be mirrored in the character of the person who chose it.*

What the Flowers Say

For hundreds of years flowers have been used to carry hidden messages—particularly between lovers. Traditionally, each bloom is characterized by a special meaning. Because they can pick up your own personal energy, you can use flowers to convey your thoughts or feelings. Again, by linking with a flower (see page 58), you can infuse it with your intent so, when the recipient receives your gift of a flower, it may communicate a larger vocabulary of coded meanings. Made up into a posy or bouquet, the message in each flower effectively adds up to a living document. So, next time you give someone a bunch of flowers or even a single bloom, think about the meaning you want to communicate, and see if the recipient picks up the special message that your gift conveys. To help you choose the most appropriate flowers, some well-documented meanings are set out opposite.

Anemone
Estrangement. "Your charms no longer appeal to me."

Apple Blossom
Beauty and goodness. "You are the epitome of loveliness."

Arbutus
Love. "You alone I love."

Aster
Afterthoughts. "I regret my impetuosity."

Begonia
Warning. "We are being watched."

Bell-flower
Morning. "Meet me tomorrow before noon."

Bindweed
Persistence. "You'll never be rid of me."

Blackthorn *Obstacles. "Some one is coming between us."*

Bluebell
Constancy. "I am faithful."

Broom
Devotion. "I am your faithful admirer."

Buttercup
Radiance. "Golden beauty is yours."

Camellia
Loveliness. "How radiantly lovely you are."

Camomile
Fortitude. "I admire your courage in adversity."

Carnation
An indication of feelings—
pink: *Encouragement needed.*
red: *Passionate love.*
white: *Pure affection.*

Cherry blossom
Increase. "To the ripening of our friendship."

Chrysanthemum
The state of a relationship—
bronze: *Friendship.*
red: *Reciprocated love.*
yellow: *Discouragement.*

Cornflower
Delicacy. "Your feet barely touch the ground."

Crocus
Joy of youth. "I delight in your freshness."

Cyclamen
Indifference. "Your protestations leave me unmoved."

Daffodil
Refusal. "I do not return your affections."

Daisy
Temperance. "I will give you an answer in a few days—I might learn to love you."

Dandelion
Absurdity. "Your pretensions are ridiculous."

Evening Primrose
Mute devotion. "Humbly I adore you."

Forget-me-not
Remembrance. "Think of me during my absence."

Foxglove
Shallowness. "You are not really in love."

Fritillary
Doubt. "Can I trust you?"

Fuchsia
Warning. "Beware! your lover is false."

Gardenia
Sweetness. "You are agreeable to the senses."

Geranium
What's happening?—
pink: Doubt. "Explain your actions."
scarlet: Duplicity. "I do not trust you."
white: Indecision. "I have not made up my mind."

Gladiolus
Pain. "Your words have wounded me."

Hawthorn
Hope. "I shall strive to win your love."

Honesty
Frankness. "I'm not certain about my feelings."

Honeysuckle
Plighted troth. "You have my heart."

Hyacinth
Expression of feelings—
blue: devotion.
white: admiration.

Hydrangea
Changeable. "Why are you so fickle?"

Iris
Ardor. "I am passionate about you."

Ivy
Bonds. "I feel connected to you."

Jasmine
Elegance. "You have the most marvelous taste in everything."

Lavender
Negation. "I like you very much but it is not love."

Lilac
Newness—
purple: First love.
white: Innocence.

Lily of the valley
Maidenly modesty. "Friendship is sweet."

Lobelia
Negativity—
blue: Dislike.
white: Rebuff.

Magnolia
Fortitude. "Be not discouraged, better days are coming."

Marigold
Unattractiveness—
African: Boorishness.
French: Jealousy.

Mimosa
Sensitiveness. "You are too brusque."

Narcissus
Self-love. "You love no one better than yourself."

Orange Blossom
Purity. "You are my first lover."

Orchid
Luxury. "You deserve all the riches I can lay at your feet."

Pansy
You are in my mind—
purple: Souvenirs.
white: Thoughts of love.
yellow: Remembrance.

Peony
Contrition. "I beg forgiveness."

Petunia
Proximity. "I like to be near you."

Poppy
Holding back—
red: Moderation.
white: Temporization. "I have not made up my mind."

Primrose
Dawning love. "I might learn to love you."

Rose
Expression of love—
red: Passionate love.
white: Refusal. "I don't love you."
yellow: Misplaced affection.

Rosemary
Remembrance. "Please keep me in your heart."

Snapdragon
Refusal. "Please don't trouble me anymore."

Snowdrop
Renewed attentions. "I find that I can't forget you."

Sunflower
Ostentation. "You're an absolute knock-out!"

Tigerlily
Passion. "My love knows no bounds."

Tulip
Avowal. "By this token I declare my passion."

Violet
Modesty. "Your lack of pretentiousness is pleasing."

Wallflower
Constancy. "I am yours till the end of time."

Do You *Know* What's Going to Happen?

Some people have a startling, uncanny ability to predict exactly what is about to occur; the knowledge of future events literally seems to come to them out of the blue.

Presentiment, also often known as precognition, is this strong sense that something is going to happen. This sensation is often non-specific—you may have an excited tingle of anticipation, or an uneasy feeling of apprehension. You have these feelings because your intuition is on the alert before your conscious awareness has come into play. But it's not difficult to develop and encourage the gift of precognition in yourself. The quiz below should reveal if you have known things in advance—which, if you had, may come as quite a surprise. Check those questions that have been true for you.

Enhancing Precognition

Knowing things in advance gives you that extra "edge" in all kinds of situations—whether it's dealing

A sense of things to come

If you respond "yes" to a question, check the box next to it. Add up the checks and note your score.

- ❑ Have you been in a situation where you suddenly sensed danger? Did the hairs on the back of your neck stand up?
- ❑ Has a letter made you feel happy even before you knew what it contained?
- ❑ Have you overheard people talking and had a sense of foreboding without knowing the background to their discussion?
- ❑ Have you ever had a compelling feeling that something was wrong while a friend was telling you about someone he or she had just met?
- ❑ On your way to an arranged meeting, have you ever had an uneasy sense that you should not be going there?

- ❑ After taking a test, have you been certain that you had passed/failed?
- ❑ While listening to someone talking about a future date, have you had an overwhelming sense that you would be in a specific place at that time?
- ❑ Have you "known" that something would occur that actually happened to you later?
- ❑ When you were a child did your parents or friends suggest a possible career? And did you "know" that you would do something completely different?
- ❑ Have you ever bought a raffle ticket and been sure that you were going to win before you did?

with people, or assessing events. So, once you've learned to trust your hunches and inner signals, you'll gain a positive boost to your confidence.

How do you enhance this amazing ability? Firstly, whenever you have a feeling that something will happen, always regard it as a "pay attention" alert. And in particular, if you ever sense danger or threat, trust your intuition—never ignore it.

It helps a lot if you can put these feelings into words and say them out loud. Then visualize the outcome in graphic detail, as if it has already happened. Once you've got the full picture, write it in your psychic diary—and keep regular notes of every "hunch" you have about people, or events. Check later whether these were accurate.

Another good intuition-sharpening technique is to do ESP exercises in telepathy (see page 50). Eventually, you'll be able to listen to your inner voice without devaluing your ability to reason.

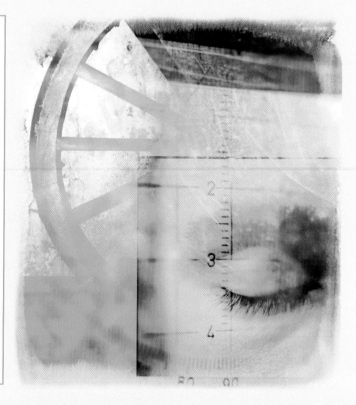

How many questions did you check?

❑ **1–3**

If you answered "yes" to even a few questions, you're already equipped with the basic ability to experience precognition.

❑ **4–6**

Learn to trust your hunches and feelings—you've more than average sensitivity to useful "out of the blue" information.

❑ **6–10**

Perhaps you should consider taking psychic development classes, as you are in touch with extra-sensory skills that could be successfully developed.

Exploring the Collective Unconscious

The psychologist Carl Jung believed that getting in touch with powerful universal images helps your inner self to function harmoniously with your conscious mind, while keeping you in tune with the cosmic world. This is a profoundly healthy state for anyone to be in, not only if you want to become an accomplished psychic but also if you want to be happier and more insightful at all times.

Jung found that various mythical and archetypal figures appeared in his patients' dreams and waking fantasies. He also knew that these feature in myths and legends around the globe. These figures can be equated with the major arcana cards of the tarot (see page 84). He suggested that archetypes emerge from a vast "data base" of human knowledge and called this the "collective unconscious." This is a very powerful resource as it serves as a connection among people of the world.

Jung's experience of working with such images persuaded him that using archetypes can trigger intuitive insights that surpass reasoned analysis; this then allows us to better understand the actions and motives of others. His method of "active imagination" decribed below stimulates this creative process.

WALKING WITH ARCHETYPES

The imaginary journey featured here is a good example of Jung's technique. Done on your own, it is a highly effective way of boosting your intuitive powers by walking you through archetypal situations and encounters. However, if you ask others to do it as well, you'll be able to compare your "experiences" with theirs. Check your experiences with the interpretation of images on page 65. It is also a good idea to record your experiences on your journey in your psychic journal.

1 *Once in a highly relaxed, meditative state (see page 23), imagine that you have woken up on a bright sunny morning—and that you have the whole day to yourself. Suddenly, you find yourself on a road.*

2 *Start walking along the road until you come to a stretch of meadow. Relax and walk about here, feel the grass under your feet, the air on your face, the smells, sights, and sounds around you.*

3 *When you are ready, return to the road and start walking along it again. You gradually become aware that the road is becoming steeper, and that you are climbing up a mountain. Observe what the journey feels like, and when you arrive at the peak, take some time to look down from the top of the mountain to the landscape below.*

Images in your journey

Pictures in visualizations and dreams are attempts by your unconscious to speak simply. They are not intended to mislead—often the obvious meaning is the most accurate, and a series of archetypal settings act as a gateway to your mind.

Meadow *This represents nature in her beneficent aspects, the positive creative basis of life and the life of the inner child.*

Forest *The crowding trees show your dark, fearful side. Walking in the forest lets you reconcile these difficult aspects of yourself.*

Mountain *Obstacles are challenges to prove yourself. The way you climb shows you how to develop your psychic freedom.*

Chapel *This symbolizes the intimate aspects of your soul; it also shows you some possibilities for psychic transformation.*

4 *When you leave, and you walk along the road again, you realize that the trees seem to be closing in and are becoming increasingly dense. Now you discover that you are right in the middle of a forest. What does this look like and how do you react to it?*

5 *After a while the light gets stronger and brighter and the road leads you out of the forest. Further along you see a building; as you get nearer, you realize it is some kind of chapel. You decide to go inside. While you're there, pay attention to your experiences and impressions. Leave the chapel when you are ready.*

6 *Outside, the sun is shining, and you start the journey home, back to your own world. What do you see on the way, and how do you feel about yourself and your surroundings? And how do you feel when you're finally back in your own home?*

What Do Your Dreams Tell You?

Your dreams can bring you an amazing fund of insights about your inner thoughts and feelings. Researchers in sleep behavior now believe that we need to dream in order to maintain equilibrium in mind and body. Some dreams either replay the events of the previous day or enact your expectations of the next. This is your mind's way of sorting and assimilating data—rather like filing documents on your computer. Researchers know that the most vivid dreams occur three or four times a night during REM sleep (a phase marked by rapid eye movement). If you are deprived of REM sleep, your body makes up the deficit, as it depends on regular amounts for overall health. So, in addition to what dreams "mean," they also help to reduce stress, tidy mental clutter, and keep you healthy and calm.

DREAM TEMPLES

People from ancient cultures used sleep and dream interpretation for healing. They built temples with sacred sleeping chambers attended by priests and priestesses trained in dream interpretation. Each patient was given a purifying bath, massaged with sacred oils, and taken to the dream chamber. The following morning, the person described his or her dreams to the priest or priestess who analyzed and explained them in great detail. This process was repeated until the patient felt restored to health.

Journal notes: Discovering your inner vision

- A dream diary will give you great insight into your unconscious life. Keep a special notebook and pen by your bedside and use it to record your significant dreams.

- You won't remember every dream you have, but note all those that are in your waking consciousness. These dreams will act as a "database" of your inner world.

- As soon as you wake up, outline your dream in detail in your diary. Concentrate on the main images; and if there were people you know in the dream, think about what they mean to you.

- As your dream diary builds up, you will begin to notice a link between your dreams—the same ones may recur, or there may be persistent images, colors, and symbols.

- Make regular summaries: group dreams under major themes, noting their subjects, story lines, places, colors, and images.

- Your dreams will make sense over time. A friend who was undergoing therapy for fear of flying had terrifying dreams about air travel. As therapy progressed, the dreams became more benign; flying became fun rather than a source of fear.

Aspects of interpretation

Have you ever had a dream which left you completely puzzled? What did it mean? If you ask the experts, you'll find that there are several classic lines of thought—so how do you decide which interpretation is right for you? For instance, you dream that you are drowning in the sea...

A behaviorist *could view the dream as an aspect of your personality. Drowning may mean that you don't feel in control—you might be "drowning" under work demands, for example.*

A pragmatist *would ask what you did the night before. Did you see a TV program on disasters at sea? It is likely that a vivid image is lodged in your memory.*

A Freudian *would link the dream to sexual wish fulfilment. Drowning is symbolic of being overwhelmed by sexual passion.*

A Jungian *regards the sea as an image of the collective unconscious. A drowning dream would indicate that you are in touch with the world at a spiritual level.*

Who is right? Don't dismiss a viewpoint without giving it some thought. These approaches all have an internal logic, so keep an open mind. As a final arbiter, use your intuition to discover what your dream is saying. When you reach the "right" meaning you will feel an "Aha!" sense of recognition.

Dream Meaning

You probably have experienced various kinds of predictive symbols in your dreams. Possibly, in your family, there are images that have particular recognized meanings. For example, if a member of the household dreams of a picture falling off the wall, it may be commonly assumed by the relatives that someone will be leaving home. But the next door neighbors may interpret this as the impending death of a family member.

Some people dream of an event just before it occurs—many individuals claimed they had "seen" President Kennedy's assassination in a dream a day or two before it happened. It is as if the shock waves of a traumatic event reverberate through time giving a glimpse of the future. But don't assume that every bad dream is going to come true.

Use common sense when interpreting dreams: some of the meanings of the dream symbols given here may be unfamiliar to you, but they reflect the experiences of psychic interpreters. Use them simply as guidelines. For instance, if you dream of a road, look at what is going on. If the road is open, free and easy to travel, your life journey will be unimpeded. But if it is full of obstacles, you will have difficulties. Also pay attention to the overall atmosphere: clean, clear, and bright elements suggest positive outcomes while dirty, broken, or decaying features point to negative situations.

Accident *A confusing situation requiring thought and discretion.*

Aircraft *Ambition and courage.*

Anchor *Resolution of present worries.*

Angels *A fortunate omen.*

Animals—
domestic: *Happiness.*
wild: *Treachery and cruelty.*

Ants *Increased industry, prosperity and expansion of business.*

Baby *New beginnings.*

Bath—
warm water: *Failure through laziness.*
cold water: *Success and prosperity.*
empty: *Warning against decisions made in anger.*

Blood *Hard but rewarding work.*

Boat *Change of residence or a journey.*

Book *Discoveries.*

Bridge *An indication of change.*

Cage—
full of birds: *Good omen.*
empty: *Loss of opportunity through carelessness.*

Cave *Rumors.*

Church—
outside: *A good omen.*
inside: *Impending trouble.*

Clock *Business worries.*

Cross *Hardwon joy and triumph.*

Crown *Accolades and honors.*

Cut finger *Recent damage.*

Dagger *Strife, enmity.*

Dancing *Joyful anticipation.*

Death *News of a birth.*

Devil *Approaching danger and temptation.*

Dove *Peace and prosperity.*

Dragon *Change of residence.*

Eagle *Realized ambitions.*

Eating *Strife between friends.*

Eggs *Innovative ideas.*

Elephant *New and influential friends.*

Eyes *Anticipated true love.*

Face *A reflection of yourself.*

Fire *Impending trouble.*

Fish *Fertility.*

Flowers *A surprise (see pages 80–81 for specific flowers).*

Forest *Shadows and fears.*

Fruits *Abundance.*

Garden *A happy marriage.*

Giant *Very lucky omen.*

Grass *Success and fertility.*

Grave *Health for the sick.*

Hair *Good health.*

Head *Misfortune.*

Hill *Realization of ambitions.*

Horse *True friendship.*

House *Domestic comfort.*

Ice *Failure in business or the end of a romance.*

Journey *There will be a journey in real life.*

Jumping *Triumph over obstacles.*

Key—
single key: *Love.*
many keys: *Prosperity without affection.*

King *Assistance from a rich and powerful friend.*

Knife *Illness, loss of money, or quarrels with relations.*

Ladder *Success.*

Lake *Comfort and freedom.*

Letter *A letter or message needs sending.*

Lightning *Inspiration or spiritual awareness.*

Lion *Power.*

Medal *Timidity and weakness on your part.*

Money *Fortunate omen, especially for those engaged in lawsuits.*

Moon *Happiness in love.*

Mouse *Interference by others in your affairs. Are you a man or a ...?*

Mouth *Expected wealth.*

Nest *Domestic happiness.*

Nut *Warning of extravagance.*

Oak *Very good omen. Calm and untroubled life.*

Ocean—
rough: *Disturbance.*
calm: *Reconciliation between two friends.*

Owl *Wisdom.*

Parents *Joy.*

Pictures *An image of you.*

Prison *Freedom.*

Pyramid *A very lucky omen.*

Queen *Profit and prosperity as a result of hard work.*

Rain *Domestic trouble.*

Rainbow *Health and wealth.*

Rat *Secret and powerful enemies.*

Ring *An important new friendship.*

Road *Your life's journey.*

Shield *Honor and fame.*

Skeleton *Comfort from unexpected quarters.*

Snow *Good news and gain.*

Spider *A lucky escape from an accident.*

Stones *Visit from a relative.*

Sun *Advancement and success.*

Swan *Happiness and psychic ability.*

Sword *Unhealthy situation that could affect you adversely.*

Table *Domestic happiness.*

Teeth *Sign of major changes, particularly if extracted or falling out.*

Tiger *Warning of someone with harmful intent.*

Tower *Great gains or great losses.*

Uniform *A journey full of adventure.*

Valley *A meeting with an old friend.*

Veil *Revelation of a secret.*

Wall *Obstacles and danger.*

War *Peace and success.*

Wasp *Envious enemies.*

Watch *Dependency.*

Window *Reconciliation after a quarrel.*

Zoo *Profitable change of employment.*

Can You Control Your Dreams?

When you don't know what to do about a problem, you may decide to "sleep on it." This phrase is a good example of how ancient wisdom has percolated into common speech. It has long been known that the answer to a baffling question may occur during sleep. A variant of this is known as lucid dreaming: when this happens you are perfectly aware that you are dreaming, and can deliberately alter details that occur in your dream. For instance, if you are dreaming about an aggressive Rotweiler, you could turn it into a pacific Chihuahua.

Primitive peoples regarded lucid dreams as an important route into the spirit world. Individuals who were able to access this dream state were often chosen to be the shamans of a tribe.

Scientists at Stanford University's sleep laboratory have offered various clues about how and when lucid dreaming occurs. The dreamer often becomes lucid while in the middle of a dream. Perhaps because something extraordinary happens, the person suddenly recognizes that he or she is in a dream. Another common trigger is returning to REM sleep after being woken up in the middle of an episode taking place in a vivid dream. Test subjects gave prearranged signals (such as fist clenching) to signal that they were in a lucid dream.

DREAM WORKS

Sleep can be a source of dazzling inspiration—many breakthroughs happen during dreams.

- *Tartini, a violinist in eighteenth-century Italy, was reputed to have made a pact with Satan; he dreamed that he was visited by the devil and played a piece "more ravishing than anything he had ever heard." The following morning he wrote out the complex sonata of his dream and called it* The Devil's Trill.

- *Robert Louis Stevenson used a lucid dreaming technique to literally "dream up" his exciting adventure stories.*

- *The poet Coleridge claimed that his poem* Kubla Khan *was a "vision in a dream."*

DIRECTING YOUR DREAMS

People vary in how vividly they dream, and how successfully they can redirect a dream's story line. With practice you can learn the technique of lucid dreaming.

1 *In the morning, start planning your dream in dramatic, colorful detail.*

2 *Return to your dream story at frequent intervals during the day and go over its details repeatedly, until the entire sequence is fixed in your consciousness.*

3 *Just before you go to sleep, relax, then replay your dream in your mind. Tell yourself with complete conviction that you intend to be conscious while you are dreaming.*

4 *If this disturbs your sleep try the following. As soon as you wake up in the morning and are in a half doze, "will" yourself to have a lucid dream, then go back to sleep.*

Insider info LUCID DREAMING

Use it to enhance mood and supply the thrill of adventure. *One of the most popular, playful activities in a lucid dream is that of flying. The sense of release, freedom, and pleasure this gives is unforgettable. Lucid dreaming also can help you to dispel nightmares. You redirect the "plot" of your nightmare so that the horror is confronted and transformed into something harmless. This is a great way of conquering fear and boosting confidence.*

If you have trouble making decisions, *lucid dreaming can help you visualize what a job, vacation, or new home could have in store. It will enable you to experience working* somewhere or being in a new location. You will react to these various situations in your dreams—are you happy, frightened, worried?

The effects of positive visualization on body and mind *are well established. Lucid dreaming can be used to overcome stress, phobias, and grief, and also to facilitate physical healing. Some enthusiasts have spotted the potential for helping stroke victims recover neuromuscular function through lucid dream imagery in which they "see" themselves moving, walking, and talking normally.*

Travel to Other Worlds in Your Dreams

Psychics can be highly aware of the astral body, the invisible subtle structure that acts as a bridge between the physical world and the world of spirit. When you are awake the astral body is superimposed onto your physical form; however, as you fall asleep, the astral body loosens and separates an inch or two away from your physical body.

During sleep, the astral body of a living person is sometimes able to cross into the spirit world—this is called an astral dream and feels so "real" it becomes super-real. Here, you may meet a loved one who has died; you have a powerful feeling that he or she is physically present. You can literally hear, see, smell, and even taste during the dream. On waking you will probably feel profoundly comforted and will remember this experience very clearly.

Insider info ASTRAL TRAVEL

You might encounter other beings—*people report meetings with wise teachers. These beings may reveal the deeper aspects of your life, or long-forgotten wisdom.*

Things are experienced differently *on the astral plane; energy follows thought with unusual speed—you only have to think of a place and you're there. And any image that enters your mind will materialize instantly.*

It can change your life. *The sensation of being outside your body gives you a sweeping, panoramic perspective—this can be liberating and calming, providing you with a wider perspective. Visiting the astral worlds during sleep gives you a good idea of what the spirit world is about and reassures you of the continuity of life.*

ATTEMPTING ASTRAL TRAVEL

1 When in a completely relaxed state (see page 23), focus carefully on where you want to go and what you want to achieve, and why. Make sure you're in a safe place and lock the door. You'll also want to be psychically protected from any negative experiences, and you can do this by calling upon a spirit guide or guardian to assist you in your astral journey. Project a positive message asking for the highest, greatest good. Make your request clear and concise.

2 Close your eyes. Concentrate on a repetitive sound—a mantra, rhythmic drumming or chanting. You should be relaxed but mentally alert. Visualize a trap door some distance away and hurl yourself against it. The door represents the pineal door of the third eye.

3 If you succeed in "escaping," you will be surrounded with golden light and, as long as you don't fall into a deep sleep, you can step out of your physical body as easily as if you were

climbing out of bed. You will be aware that your mind is awake but your body still sleeps.

4 Once you are on the astral plane just let yourself go to wherever the spirit guides you. It will take some time to acclimatize yourself, so just accept what happens.

5 You will automatically return to your normal state when ready. Immediately note down your travel experiences in your dream diary.

Is Your Pet Psychic?

Domestic pets often have an uncanny psychic ability to anticipate their owners' thoughts, moods and actions. The most common example is the family dog that goes to the front door just before its owner arrives and sits expectantly, tail wagging. This even happens when the owner has deliberately varied his or her arrival time in order to "test" a pet's ESP. Cats have similar predictive talents, and many riders say their horses know when they are approaching the stable. Cage birds, too, often hop up and down on their perches in excitement just before their owners comes home. Your own pet may have similar abilities—have a look at the quiz on page 75 to find out more.

In addition to possible psychic powers, it's now well recognized that pets also have positive health benefits. Domestic animals can make good therapists. People who find they can't talk to other humans about their problems, often find it easier to confide in a pet. There's great comfort in their loving, non-judgmental attention.

Animal owners generally enjoy better health than non-owners. Heart patients are known to live longer when they have a pet, and tests have shown that high blood pressure drops to a healthy level when a pet is around. Caring for animals calms stress, and just being with them reduces anxiety. That is why dentists often have fish tanks in their waiting rooms.

Incredible journeys

Nowadays families move home frequently; some people think it is best to find a new home for a pet rather than upsetting it by taking it far away from its familiar territory. Most pets settle down, but others have different ideas, and travel hundreds of miles in search of their owner.

This happened to a New York veterinarian who got a new job 2,000 miles across the USA in California. He decided to give his cat to his friends and set off to establish his West Coast

practice. Six months after he'd arrived, his cat walked in through the door. There was no mistaking the identity of this particular creature; he quickly checked it for a slight deformation on its tail—it was there, as he expected. He had treated the injury (the result of a bite) when the cat was a tiny kitten.

Although no-one really knows how animals can track owners with such accuracy, some parapsychologists regard this ability as a form of "remote viewing" (see page 54).

Rate your pet's ESP

❑ 1 Does your pet seem to understand your moods and feelings?

❑ 2 When you have made an appointment to take it to the vet, does it disappear?

❑ 3 Has it spent hours looking at a wall, seemingly watching something that isn't there?

❑ 4 Does it howl or hide during a seance or other psychic happening?

❑ 5 Is it always at the door to meet you, whatever time you return home?

❑ 6 Does it becomes more affectionate when you're in a bad mood?

❑ 7 When someone it knows calls, does your pet nuzzle the phone?

❑ 8 Just as you think about taking the dog for a walk, does it get excited?

If you answered "yes" to numbers

1 6 7
Your pet may have healing skills.

2 5 8
Telepathy is your pet's speciality.

3 4
This shows that your pet is sensitive to spirit presences.

PSYCHIC TOOLS

3

Would You Recognize True Love?

Astrologers believe that the stars have a strong impact on your life. This correlates with the psychic's understanding that all matter is linked by a unifying energy. If you're looking for true love, you may have explored astrology to find out the star sign that is most compatible with yours. While there's no way that complex relationships can be generalized into twelve categories of attraction and suitability, don't give up on the zodiac completely. It may prove to be a surprisingly good psychic matchmaker.

Your birth chart provides the key: as well as defining your character, it also spotlights the qualities in others that attract and complement yours. The saying, "men are from Mars and women are from Venus" has true astrological validity; their positions in your birth chart are highly significant to your love life.

YOUR IDEAL PARTNER

Mars and Venus will appear in particular zodiac signs in your birth chart. If you're a woman, check where Mars is located and if you're a man, look for Venus in your chart. Refer to the table (right) for the qualities you would expect to find in a male or female of the particular sign. Each sign is affiliated to one of four elements: Earth, Fire, Air, or Water. You're mostly at ease around those with the same energy influences, but opposite elements can be harmonious, too. Air and Fire signs feel comfortable with each other, as do Earth and Water.

Earth signs

TAURUS
Tactile, sensual, loyal, relaxed, easygoing, patient, practical. Likes to be invited and feel wanted.

VIRGO
Focused, skillful, intelligent, clean, discerning, sincere. Wishes to be heard, respected, and trusted.

CAPRICORN
Ambitious, wise, understanding, responsible, disciplined. Needs respect and to be allowed to organize.

Fire signs

ARIES
Active, assertive, independent, leading, expressive, energetic. Needs self-expression and independence.

LEO
Playful, creative, fun, hearty, passionate. Demands to be loved and appreciated.

SAGITTARIUS
Adventurous, honest, knowledgeable. Requires honesty in others and benefits from adventures.

Air signs

GEMINI

Intellectually curious, communicative, light, spontaneous, playful, witty. Needs to communicate and be regarded as interesting.

LIBRA

Charming, diplomatic, romantic, polite, considerate. Wants romance and caring consideration.

AQUARIUS

Exciting, different, rebellious, friendly, compassionate. Demands the freedom to be him/herself.

Water signs

CANCER

Caring, affectionate, loving, sensitive, protective. Craves affection and needs leeway to be moody.

SCORPIO

Passionate, feeling, deep, loving, loyal, empathetic. Must be deeply emotionally expressive.

PISCES

Trusting, intuitive, sensitive, mediumistic, peaceful, imaginative. Asks for trust in return and to be given space.

Insider info BIRTH CHARTS

Each person's chart is unique *and provides information that no other source can. Although fairly easy to construct, their complex interweaving energies are much harder to interpret. Charts are available by mail order or on the internet; you'll need to know the place, date, and time of your birth.*

To assess the Venus/Mars influence, *you'll need to find the position of Venus or Mars in your birth chart (depending on whether you're a man or a woman) then, refer to the keywords under the relevant sign to discover what qualities you should seek in a partner. Think about your important relationships. Did partners you were happiest with exhibit a large number of these qualities? Did failed relationships, or difficult ones, lack the qualities indicated as necessary for a good relationship?*

A person's rising sign or ascendant is important. *It governs the way we express ourselves. Therefore, if you know when your partner was born, check his or her rising sign, or ascendant, as it will be a major influence on him or her.*

Attraction is not always automatic. *Although the sign occupied by Venus or Mars is a good indicator for happy relationships, it does not necessarily mean that people born under that sign will be your best match. It merely says that the qualities of that sign will need to be present.*

Accessing the Wisdom of the I Ching

The I Ching, a profound psychic tool that has been in use for over 3,000 years, imparts celestial wisdom from the ancient spirits of heaven and earth. The more you use the I Ching for your intuitive development, the more you'll appreciate its profound subtlety. You'll find that it gives you unusual insights, not just about complex areas of self-growth but also practical, day-to-day problems.

The I Ching's messages are relayed through 64 hexagrams, configurations that hold an entire system of thought based on the Chinese concept of yin and yang. It teaches that the aim of life is to achieve and keep a balance. Yin and yang represent core male and female principles: the male or active energy of yang inspires you to have an idea, impose your will and take action; the female receptive energy of yin enables you to go with the flow and adapt to events.

BUILDING YOUR HEXAGRAMS

Use the following method to construct your six-lined figure; then you can interpret its meaning.

1 *Formulate your question clearly in your mind. If you're not happy in your job, for example, you may want to know if you are in the right one or if another would make you happier. Think of it as you sit at a table or other flat surface with a notebook and pencil ready for use.*

2 *Choose three coins of similar size and shape with clearly defined heads and tails. Heads represent the yang or unbroken line (———) and tails signify a yin or broken line (— —).*

3 *Focus on your question and throw the coins onto the table six times in succession. A majority of heads makes a yang line; mostly tails a yin line.*

4 *Write down each line, starting from the bottom up. Repeat the procedure until you have a stack of six lines. This is your hexagram—the I Ching's response to your question.*

5 *Look up your hexagram and its meaning from the list on the following pages and keep a note of the questions and answers in your psychic journal.*

6 *If you asked whether you should change your job, and you threw 63 Fording Now or 5 Caution, the former would be affirmative, the latter negative. Other answers, like 50 The Vessel may be less immediately obvious. Use your intuition to connect the given meaning with your own thoughts and instincts.*

1 Creative action *You are confronted with many obstacles—it is a time to take action. Use persuasion rather than force.*

 2 Letting go *Join with others but don't shirk responsibilities. Quietly accept, cherish everything and help it grow.*

 3 Gestation *Allow matters to evolve. Chaos precedes a new venture. New ideas are beginning to form.*

 4 Growth *Your understanding is dull and clouded through youthful folly. Wait and learn.*

 5 Caution *A time for waiting—there could be danger ahead. Go slowly, especially in love. Watch for the right time.*

 6 Arguing *This is not a harmonious time, it is full of contrary people and ideas. Compromise if necessary.*

 7 Discipline *A time to put things in order. Seek people of experience and authority.*

8 Alliance *Mutual support. Discard old ideas and find new ways to regroup your affairs. Change must come now.*

9 Gradual accumulation *Adapt to whatever comes along. Take the long view on life. Be flexible and adaptable.*

10 Treading *Find and make your own way. Persevere in your efforts to create a profound change.*

11 Pervading *Great abundance and harmony. Stay resolute within and adaptable with others. Peace is at hand.*

12 Obstruction *Blocked communications and obstacles. Stagnation. A dead-end situation and a period of isolation. It is not your fault.*

13 Harmony *A communal life with common causes or shared interests with those who combine their talents and efforts.*

14 Abundance *You have great power to achieve success. Concentrate your inner force to create joy.*

15 Humbling *Abandon pride and arrogance. Keep your words and actions simple. Taking lower positions will bring success.*

16 Awareness *Be ready to respond. Build up your strength and resources to prepare for whatever the future will bring.*

 17 Following *Go with the flow. Be guided by the way life is moving. Everything has its season.*

18 Corruption *Decay and hidden poison. Slovenliness, laziness, and weakness must be fought against. Prepare carefully for changes.*

19 Arrival of the new *A situation that is evolving and progressing. Possible promotion or advancement.*

20 Vigilance *See other's true motivations and show your own. Contemplate—let everything come into view.*

21 Biting through *Confront your problems. Be tenacious—know you have made the right decision and stick to it.*

 22 Grace *Show your true self. External forms are ephemeral and illusory.*

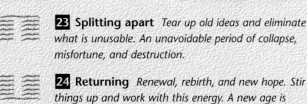

23 Splitting apart *Tear up old ideas and eliminate what is unusable. An unavoidable period of collapse, misfortune, and destruction.*

24 Returning *Renewal, rebirth, and new hope. Stir things up and work with this energy. A new age is beginning.*

25 Innocence *Disentangle yourself, be spontaneous, free from ulterior motives. Trust your instinct and follow your conscience.*

26 Power of the great *Focus on the highest ideas—this is a time for great effort and achievement. Learn through experience.*

27 Nourishment *Feed both your earthly and spiritual body for complete well being.*

28 Excess *Hold onto your ideals. A plan will bring profit and insight. Do not be afraid to act alone.*

29 Abyss *Unavoidable danger. Take the plunge and face your fear. Now is the time to concentrate and take risks.*

30 Radiance *Light, warmth, and spreading awareness. Combine high values, noble principles and intellect, logic, and good sound ideas.*

31 Conjoining *Stimulation and excitement. A good time to marry. Accept and submit to the female—yin brings birth and renewal.*

32 Persevering *Endurance is the way to acquire a powerful character. Act in the long term to attain objectives.*

33 Retiring *Withdraw and conceal yourself. Deal with the situation from a distance—the surrounding circumstances are not favorable.*

34 Strength *Power must be implemented gently and with moderation. Renounce violence.*

35 Prospering *Progress in a changing situation. Take a new view of yourself.*

36 Hidden brightness *Protect yourself and accept a difficult task. Conflicts must be faced even if you cannot solve them.*

37 Family *Nourish and support the family—this will bring illumination. Use clear language to connect with your relatives.*

38 Discord *Make an effort to eliminate conflict. Avoid people and situations that clash and react against each other.*

39 Difficulties *Confront obstacles—they will point out the course to take so that you can progress and be free from troubles.*

40 Loosening *Resolve a difficulty by disentangling problems one by one. This will bring relief or deliverance.*

41 Diminishing *Something will be revealed showing that sacrifice is needed. Tone things down and show restraint and moderation.*

42 Augmenting *A rewarding situation overflowing with abundance and possibilities. Increase without limits.*

43 Breakthrough *Face disorder with speed and resolution, while controlling your passions. Use firmness, adaptability, and kindness.*

44 Coupling *The opening influence of yin. Sexual intercourse and marriage. For true union respect social rules and principles.*

45 **Clustering** *A large number of people can work together with the same objective and motivation, but they must be organized.*

 46 **Ascending** *Lift yourself to a higher level through your own efforts. Amass small things to achieve the great.*

 47 **Oppression** *You are cut off—this is a moment of truth. Turn inward and find a way to open communication.*

 48 **The well** *Interact with others. A situation of potentially inexhaustible resources and possibilities is open to all.*

 49 **Renewal** *Another layer or facade is removed as part of a natural process. For improvements, revolution must occur.*

 50 **The vessel** *Discover your inner qualities and the correct way to use them for spiritual and material transformation. Exercise free will.*

51 **Shake** *Wake up! Start all over again—spring has come. It will bring storms but they will clear the air and enable new beginnings.*

52 **Stillness** *The calm of the mountain. Seek stability by surrendering your desires, fears, speculations, and fantasies.*

53 **Gradual advance** *Progress must be slow, so learn to proceed step by step, without angst.*

54 **Converting the maiden** *Realize your hidden potential for passion or desire. Marriage of a younger sister or daughter.*

 55 **Plenty** *A time of affluence, profusion, and generosity. Use this advantage sparingly so that it lasts.*

56 **Exile** *Wandering far away from home. A restless situation is uncertain, but there may also be wonderful potential.*

57 **Gently penetrating** *Be supple and flexible. Let yourself be shaped by events. Don't impose your will but never lose sight of your purpose.*

 58 **Joy** *Good humor and a positive attitude bring pleasure to life. Be sympathetic to all through communication and self-expression.*

59 **Dispersing** *Clear the decks. Now is the time to start a new project or found an enterprise—but keep things fluid.*

60 **Limitation** *Learn to walk the middle path to give your life a measured form. Play by the rules now.*

61 **The center** *This is the power of a free heart without prejudice or judgment. Inner truth is always within—just listen.*

62 **Small scale** *A time of subtle transition resulting in the triumph of the soul. Whatever the moment forces you to do is right for now.*

63 **Fording now** *Everything is ready for you to proceed. Be vigilant at all times and pay attention to detail to avoid mistakes.*

64 **Not yet fording** *Important change is imminent—gather your energy for the right moment. Be objective and don't be blinded by enthusiasm.*

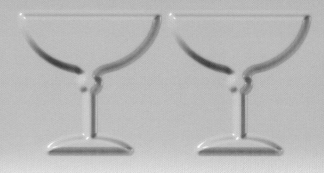

Reading the Tarot

The tarot pack opens up a miniature, mysterious world, full of portentous symbols with significant meanings. The reader lays out the cards in different combinations to explore the past, present, and future. A tarot pack has 78 cards. 56 of the cards are the minor arcana; these are similar to ordinary playing cards and consist of four suits with court cards. 22 of the cards are the major arcana; they feature archetypal images that illustrate various stages of spiritual growth.

If you want to get the best from the tarot, take time to examine various decks, and let your intuition tell you which is right for you. There also are many reference books with "interpretations" of the cards—again, you'll discover those that resonate with your own sense of their meanings (not surprising as the tarot symbols are tied into the collective unconscious, see page 64). But follow your own hunches even if they contradict received wisdom; this is an example of your intuition at work.

THE MINOR ARCANA CARDS
Whether you're reading for yourself or someone else, the person asking a question of the tarot is called "the inquirer." Take plenty of time to study the cards and their network of associations. Meditate on each one, and use them in simple spreads at first (see right). Let the interplay between images inspire your intuition as you build your interpretation. But never use the tarot when you are upset or traumatized—your negative vibrations will almost certainly give you an incorrect reading.

Cups

ISSUES	*Emotions and love issues*
TIME	*Spring/days*
ELEMENT	*Water*

KING, QUEEN, KNIGHT, AND PAGE OF CUPS
These cards represent a blond, warm-hearted person full of good intentions. It may be the man or woman the inquirer loves.

ASTROLOGICAL SIGNS
Cancer, Scorpio, or Pisces.

Swords

ISSUES	*Illness or difficulties*
TIME	*Summer/months*
ELEMENT	*Air*

KING, QUEEN, KNIGHT, AND PAGE OF SWORDS
These indicate a person with dark brown coloring who has power over people—possibly a manipulator who is not always honest.

ASTROLOGICAL SIGNS
Gemini, Libra, or Aquarius.

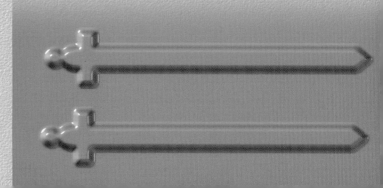

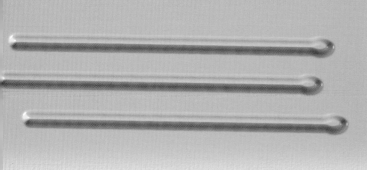

Wands

ISSUES   *Family and business concerns*

TIME   *Autumn/weeks*

ELEMENT *Fire*

KING, QUEEN, KNIGHT, AND PAGE OF WANDS
If you choose one of these cards, it signifies a fair-haired, friendly, sympathetic, family centered person who can help you.

ASTROLOGICAL SIGNS
Aries, Leo, or Sagittarius.

Pentacles

ISSUES   *Money or material matters*

TIME   *Winter/years*

ELEMENT *Earth*

KING, QUEEN, KNIGHT, AND PAGE OF PENTACLES
This may point to someone wealthy with dark hair and eyes who can materially help the inquirer.

ASTROLOGICAL SIGNS
Taurus, Virgo, or Capricorn.

A SIMPLE TAROT SPREAD

1 *Use only the minor arcana cards and pick out a court card that matches the inquirer. For instance, a blond woman from a water sign would choose the Queen of Cups. This is the significator, the center of the spread.*

2 *The inquirer shuffles the cards for a few minutes then cuts them with the left hand. Seven cards are set out left to right, with the fourth card on top of the significator.*

3 *The first three cards relate to the past; the fourth, lying on the significator, relates to present circumstances; and the last three indicate the outcome and future possibilities.*

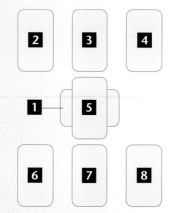

The next step in using the tarot is to include the 22 major arcana cards in your spreads. These are believed to hold a powerful code of occult wisdom dating back over 3,000 years to the sacred rituals of ancient Egyptian priests. The images of the major arcana are "archetypes" (see page 64), and help you to connect with the deeper meaning underlying events and people in your life.

0 The Fool
Listen to all: everything has meaning and everyone is your guide.

1 The Magician
This reminds you that your thoughts have power. Monitor your ideas and think positively.

2 The High Priestess
The nature of life is change: accept this and trust your own intuition. Do not be afraid of hidden secrets.

3 The Empress
The archetypal woman—let her understanding stabilize and guide you. Look at your female aspects. Are they happily balanced?

4 The Emperor
The man of authority, strength, courage, and will. Examine your male aspects and balance them with your inner female side.

5 The Hierophant or Pope
Listen to your inner voice for divine inspiration, wisdom, and truth.

6 The Lovers
You are connected to the inspirational and spiritual forces of love.

7 The Chariot
Take the reins of your life and start to control its true direction.

8 Justice
The laws of cause and effect are eternal—nobody is exempt.

9 The Hermit
After a period of retreat to contemplate inner illumination, understanding and truth must be shared with others.

10 The Wheel
Without movement life stagnates. Let go of the past and look to the future: everything is part of an endless learning process.

ASK YOUR ARCHETYPE
If you are troubled, shuffle the major arcana cards, silently asking for the archetype that will help you. When the cards feel warm in your hands, cut them into two piles. Take the card on the top of the lower pile. Meditate on this image; let it come alive and bring you insight, wisdom, and calm.

11 Strength

No one faces anything that they can't handle. Hardships build up your spiritual muscle.

12 The Hanged Man

Is your sacrifice really necessary, or is it simply an excuse not to be responsible for your life? Be brave and follow your inner truth.

13 Death

In death there is also birth. And on the higher levels there is no death, only movement and change.

14 Temperance

Wisdom and restraint are needed. The flowing healing waters of time will nourish you, supplementing your deficiencies.

15 The Devil

Instead of listening to the quiet, still voice of love you hear the voice of fear. Look the devil directly in the eye. Only then will he vanish.

16 The Tower

A brilliant flash of lightning reveals the problems that you have ignored. Search for a more balanced, healthy existence.

17 The Star

Life is exacting and will give you the lessons you need in no uncertain terms. Illumination is the outcome but hope is always present.

18 The Moon

Only a fool would say they are never wrong. Know and forgive yourself as you really are and walk on.

19 The Sun

True success comes with application. Everything on the material plane is transitory—only your inner being is immortal.

20 Judgment

Like the phoenix rising from the ashes, you will emerge triumphant.

21 The World

When all energies are aligned, everything becomes possible. At the same time, you realize that all your needs are met and you want for nothing.

The simplest way to read the cards is to pay heed to their surface meanings—try asking what the symbols suggest to you. Or, you can study the arrangement of the cards and see how action might develop—what is going to happen over the course of the next year. Lastly, in looking at a layout, you begin to become aware of insights never before experienced—you suddenly realize your life has followed a particular pattern—you've never had a satisfactory relationship with anyone and now you can see why.

As your confidence builds, you should develop a sense of dynamic psychic connection with the cards and begin to try more complex spreads. The Celtic Cross (see right), is a helpful example. If you find that you have a natural empathy with the tarot, make good use of it. A psychic tool that resonates in close harmony with your intuition and imagination is immensely helpful in all areas of your life—from your emotional relationships to professional and leisure pursuits.

Improving your tarot reading skills

The "inquirer" is the person seeking answers—whether you're reading for yourself or someone else, study each card and talk through your responses and impressions.

If the majority of the cards are from the major arcana, powerful outside forces may be at work.

If several court cards appear, this suggests that many people are involved.

If the tenth card is a court card, the outcome will depend on someone else's influence.

If you feel that the last card does not make sense, remove it and go through the whole process again, using this card as the significator.

Use the outcome card in your meditations and thoughts, especially before going to sleep, and ask for enlightenment about your question.

If you draw the major arcana card "the Moon" in the first position, put the cards away—you will not get an effective spread now. Try again in 24–48 hours.

THE CELTIC CROSS

This is a wonderful method of thinking about and feeling through a puzzling situation such as how should you react to a crisis arising at work or in a personal relationship.

1 *Choose a significator (card 1) to represent you as inquirer (see pages 84–85) and position it as shown below.*

2 *Shuffle the cards until they feel warm in your hands. Cut with the left hand and set out as shown here.*

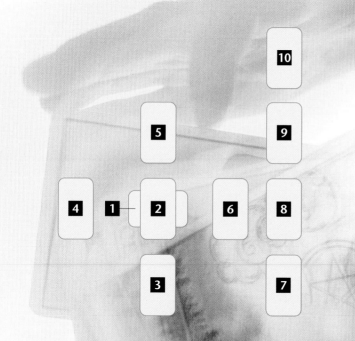

1 This covers the inquirer, relating to the general situation and influences.

2 This crosses the inquirer, warning of any opposing forces whether they are positive or negative.

3 This is beneath the inquirer; it is the basis of the matter, showing something that may have come to light.

4 This is behind the inquirer, pointing to what has just occurred or is beginning to pass away.

5 This crowns the inquirer, representing a possible influence that may or may not come about.

6 This is before the inquirer, revealing the influences that will operate in the near future.

7 This explores fears and any negative feelings around the situation.

8 This uncovers the opinions and influences of friends and family.

9 This reveals the inquirer's own hopes and ideas on the subject.

10 This suggests a possible outcome, drawn from the influences of the other cards.

Developing Clairvoyant Vision

If you've ever consulted a traditional clairvoyant, he or she may have described various images seen while gazing into a crystal ball. This shining object is the tool of the professional seer or scryer—ancient names for a clairvoyant—a person who "sees clearly." The psychic art of seeing images of past, present, and future events can be yours, too; learning it gives you a special insight into what's happening in your world, and a picture of how events will turn out for you and others.

If you want to develop your clairvoyant skills, you don't need go to the trouble and expense of buying a crystal ball. People have been scrying for thousands of years, using all sorts of reflective surfaces including dark pools of water or ink, clear or colored marbles, pieces of coal, jet or onyx, polished metal—in fact just about anything that helps to focus and attune psychic vision. Pure quartz crystal is known to intensify psychic energies and makes a particularly good scrying tool.

Scrying requires enormous patience and an exact level of relaxation. The surface you use acts as a doorway into time and space, and gazing into it produces a light hypnotic trance. This allows you to "see" information arriving in the form of pictures, symbols, letters, impressions, and sensations, which appear generally in answer to a question that you or another puts forward.

Guidelines to clarity

The symbol you see may mean different things depending on circumstance. A cat may mean good luck in one situation (you'll land on your feet) and act as a warning in another (you're thinking about someone who may or may not be a friend). As you gain in experience, recording your visions and what comes to pass, you'll learn to combine your intuition with an observant and open mind.

Your character and the issues that interest you will strongly affect the meaning of any images. For example, the symbol of scales may appear. This could mean that you are involved in some kind of legal process. On the other hand, if you are doing research, it might refer to your judgment of the data. If you ask a question about spiritual matters, the scales may represent divine justice.

USING A SCRYING TOOL

1 *Work in a dimly lit spot and sit with your back to the light source. When you're scrying for someone else, he or she should sit at least an arm's length away from you.*

2 *If your scrying tool is transparent, put a small square of black velvet or other dark fabric underneath it, to help focus your vision.*

3 *Make yourself deeply relaxed, stay perfectly silent and concentrate your gaze right into the heart of your scrying surface. If nothing happens the first time, take a break. Try again in short bursts of up to 20 minutes.*

4 *You'll know when images are starting to form—the inner surface stops reflecting external pictures. It turns a milky color and this will swiftly turn black. At this point, shapes emerge.*

5 *Two kinds of images appear, and you'll need to use your intuition to interpret them. Those with direct messages reveal a scene or incident played out in front of you, as if you were watching a film. These represent actual happenings, past, present, or future. At first you'll find it difficult to determine in what time scale the images shown are happening, but trust your hunches. With practice, you'll get better at identifying this.*

6 *Other images are indirect or symbolic. They are similar to those in dreams, and you can use dream symbols as guidelines (see page 68). Again, practice and dedication will give you the confidence to interpret them accurately.*

What Can You See in the Tea Leaves?

If you've never tried divination before, the simple act of drinking a cup of tea may bring surprising revelations. You don't have to have any particular psychic ability to do it—anyone who has the patience to study symbols and their meanings can become proficient. But as with any method of divination, you shouldn't use it too often—read the leaves once or twice a week at most. Some symbols will stand out immediately; the larger the symbol, the more important and relevant it will be.

Check to see if any of the symbols are connected. If you see a human face, for example, is there an initial letter next to it that may give you a clue as to who it might be?

THE AREAS OF THE CUP
The cup's "regions" act as a psychic map for the questioner. The pictures created by the leaves are interpreted according to where they are situated.

Opposite the handle
This is the site concerning work and business.

The sides and bottom of the cup *These denote time scales: if a symbol is close to the rim, it refers to something happening soon. Images on the side of the cup are not so immediate in their impact and those on the bottom represent events a long way into the future.*

Handle *This area represents you, your home, and close family.*

THE TEA RITUAL

For a good, clear reading, buy a leaf tea which has large leaves—
China tea is ideal but other Oriental varieties are suitable too.

1 Put a tablespoon of tea in a pot and cover with boiling water. Serve it in a cup and saucer—use a plain white or light colored cup with a wide mouth.

2 Drink from the tea until about one teaspoonful is left in the cup.

3 Hold the cup in your left hand and swirl it three times in a circular anti-clockwise motion. As you do this, focus your mind on your question. Be very specific if you want good results.

4 Invert the cup onto the saucer and leave it for at least a minute, until the liquid has drained away.

5 Now turn the cup over and examine it as described above.

Should I move house now?

Here's how the leaves answered the question. The bat shape at the top of the cup over the handle covers the area concerning the home. A bat may seem ominous, but it can mean that your fears of the unknown will be banished in the light of day. A female figure at the base carries a broom. It could indicate a completely new start.

Positive symbols

Acorn, amulet, anchor, angel, ark, bees, birds, boot, bridge, bull, circle, clover, corn, cow, crown, dove, duck, eagle, elephant, fig, fish, flowers, horseshoe, ship, swan

Negative symbols

Alligator, arc, arrow, bat, black flag, coffin, cross, dagger, drum, hour glass, monkey, mouse, rat, scythe, skeleton, square, stake, sword, wreck

What Can a Person's Hands Tell You?

Classically trained palm readers study the lines, shapes, and marks on hands in remarkable detail. You may not be an expert in this sense, but you can certainly use your psychic skills to "read" hands. When someone puts his or her hand in yours, take plenty of time to psychically tune yourself into the particular energy you feel. This will be your main source of insight about that person. Any patterns and lines you see act as focal points, triggers for your intuition rather than a blueprint.

Left or Right?

There are two main opinions about the significance of the left and right hands. The traditional view is that the passive hand (left for a right-handed person and right for someone who is left-handed) is a miniature profile of innate character and potential. The features of this hand are believed to remain constant over the years, while the lines on the dominant hand change and evolve to reveal what has been achieved with any inborn aptitudes.

Modern palm readers say that the lines on both hands change, and that the hands are "cross wired" to the right and left sides of the brain, which affects the changes. The right hand shows reasoning, analytical, and logical ability, and the left reveals emotional, intuitive, and creative aspects.

Again, your intuition is your best ally here; whichever hand that you're holding, listen to the psychic messages that you pick up and trust them.

WHAT'S YOUR HAND SHAPE?

A quick glance at the shape of someone's hands can tell you a lot. There are seven major types—can you recognize which one is yours?

Square
Fingertips are flat across the top and the palm appears as high as it is broad.

You're a steady, matter-of-fact person who reaps the benefits of your own efforts.

Spatulate or active
Thickish fingers with flat tops that are short compared with the palm.

You're bold and daring, a courageous pioneer seeking to improve the lot of others.

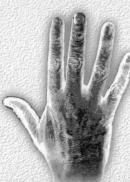

Conical or temperamental
Slender, tapering fingers slightly shorter than the palm.

Impetuous and impulsive, your mood fluctuates quickly—you get depressed about trivia.

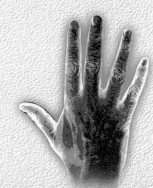

MAIN LINES

Heart, head, fate, and life lines are the key indicators. Strong, unbroken lines signify positive aspects.

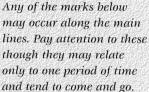

Heart Line

Head Line

Life Line

Fate Line

KEY MARKS

Any of the marks below may occur along the main lines. Pay attention to these though they may relate only to one period of time and tend to come and go.

Crosses *Shock and worries*

Squares *Restriction*

Triangles *Talent*

Star *Luck with money*

Grills and grids *Illness*

Islands *Hardships*

Chains *A line full of chains shows confusion*

Non-specific dots and pitting *Usually occur at the end of a line and indicates illness or weakness—usually temporary*

Knotty or philosophical	**Pointed, or idealistic**	**Elemental**	**Mixed**
Shortish, uneven fingers combined with a tall, slender palm.	*Very long, smooth, tapering fingers with a tall, thin palm.*	*Short, wide fingers and palm.*	*Equal-length fingers and palm.*
You're an intellectual; you love analysis using methodical, reasoning.	*A lover of art and beauty, you're an idealist but rather impractical.*	*You're practical, not intellectual. In exceptional circumstances you can be a great leader.*	*Adaptable and versatile, you're a jack-of-all trades. You may be a gifted inventor.*

What Can You Learn from the Runes?

Those gifted with rune magic are said to get their powers from Odin, the one-eyed god of the occult. If you discover that you have psychic affinity with this Scandinavian oracle, you'll derive great benefit from his mysterious powers. A single rune can be meditated upon when thinking about the answer to a problem, such as "Is now a good time to break up with my present partner?" More information, however, is gained from drawing several runes and judging how they work together. Can they point out the direction you should take in achieving your goal—when to suggest and how to manage a separation in the least painful way, for example.

Carved stone or wood runes are widely available. To make your own, collect 25 1-inch diameter round, flat pebbles. Use a marker pen, paint or nail polish to create the symbols shown below. Take plenty of time to meditate on the meaning of each rune as you decorate it; this way you will reinforce the energy within the stones. Keep runes in a roomy drawstring bag. Every time you use the runes, their vibrations become even more powerful.

The Self
Rectification comes before progress. A time of change and growth.

Partnership, a gift
True union can only occur when both parties are strong.

The Messenger
Observe what is around you. Everything has meaning for self-growth.

Retreat, inheritance
You gain through abandoning the past. Submission is required.

Strength *Just as trees drop their leaves you must give up something to allow new growth.*

Initiation, secrets
Surprises. For spiritual transformation, set aside external matters

Constraint, pain
Fears and struggles. You have restricted yourself. Pay off debts to progress.

Fertility *You can complete what you have begun. Birth is often painful—persevere.*

Defense *Delays. Be patient, relax, and wait. Quietly put your house in order.*

Protection *Don't let emotion prevail. Reason and action are the only true protection.*

SIMPLE RUNE DIVINATION

1 *Hold the bag of runes in your hand and concentrate on a question. Keep it very simple. As you do this, gently shake the runes in the bag.*

2 *When you feel you'll get an answer open the bag and put one hand inside,* moving the runes around until one stone seems to stick to your fingers. This is the one that will give you the answer to your question. See below for an interpretation of each rune's meaning.

3 *If you need a broader view, follow the same procedure but choose three runes and lay them out left to right.*

4 *The first relates to the situation, the second to any action required, and the third to the outcome or new situation.*

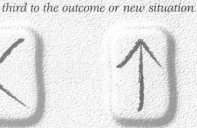

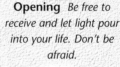

Possessions *The laws of cause and effect are clues to success. Share with others.*

Joy, light *New energy, clarity. A realigned self brings fulfilment and renewal.*

Harvest *Be patient— this is no time for speed. Know that whatever the outcome, all is well.*

Opening *Be free to receive and let light pour into your life. Don't be afraid.*

Warrior energy *The spiritual warrior uses will without attachment to the outcome.*

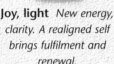

Growth *To accomplish the work modestly, patience, and kindness are required.*

Movement *You have made steady progress and gained security and self-confidence.*

Flow *Relax when the water is gentle and take action when it is choppy.*

Disruption *Things will not go to plan now. Power comes from inner strength.*

Union *This is the soul's journey, linking spirit and matter. Discard illusions.*

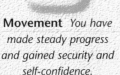

Gateway *A time for reflection. Look at the past and what you have gained. Now move on.*

Breakthrough *Darkness is behind you and everything is transformed for ever.*

Standstill *A cold atmosphere. Find what keeps you on ice and let it go to thaw out.*

Wholeness *You realize that you already possess what you seek within yourself.*

The Unknowable *A blank. Courage is needed. Inner change means emancipation.*

Using a Divining Rod

We don't really know how a piece of wood or metal can detect the presence of underground water, oil, and minerals, but people have been dowsing for thousands of years. There are various theories as to how dowsing works: one view is that humans retain some primitive tracking instinct for water that is normally dormant, but may become activated. Then there is the possibility that the divining rod emits waves of energy that are bounced back once the dowser has made a "hit." Another idea is that the dowser psychically tunes in to the energy field of hidden materials, using the divining rod to trigger the process. Whatever the explanation, it is an exciting experience for the novice psychic to feel the reaction of the dowsing tool as it responds—you feel profoundly close to living energy sources.

Today, dowsing is used as a tool by people interested in environmental health; it can help locate underground sources of water that may cause degenerative disease in the people living above.

MAKING YOUR OWN DIVINING ROD

Traditionally the divining rod is made out of a forked hazel or willow twig, but a shaped piece of metal works just as well.

1 *Find a metal coat hanger, untwist it and make it straight. Then split it into two pieces.*

2 *Bend each piece into an L shape: these are your divining rods. Now get two empty disposable ballpoint pen tubes and place one rod inside each.*

When you hold these upright the rods should have room to move freely.

3 *If you want a traditional rod, and have plenty of trees nearby, look for a hazel or willow branch that has grown into the shape of a wishbone. This makes a fine divining tool.*

NARROWING THE SEARCH

Dowsers are asked to identify many different kinds of underground materials in addition to water. They may be looking for oil or valuable minerals; seams of gold, silver, platinum, and other precious metals, or rock formations that hold diamonds and other gems. Each of these produces a slightly different reaction from the rod, so some practitioners use an ingenious method to improve their accuracy. They "pre-tune" their rods to the precise vibrations of the material they are seeking. For instance, if a dowser is searching for gold, he or she assesses the rod's reactions to a sample of gold ore. If the rod has exactly the same reaction on site, the chances of finding gold are greatly improved.

DOWSING FOR WATER

Water may be hidden deep below a piece of parched earth—can you find it?

1 *Concentrate, but remain relaxed, walk slowly and purposefully around the designated area and silently ask where you can find water.*

2 *If you're using metal rods, you'll know when there is water below the ground because the rods will move together to form a cross.*

3 *If you are dowsing with hazel or willow, hold the two wishbone sides lightly between your fingertips and walk with the single end pointing up. This end will suddenly "pull" and point downward with a strong force when you have detected underground water.*

4 *At the spot where the metal rods crossed or the wooden stick pointed down, you should make an exploratory dig for the water source.*

What Can You Do with a Pendulum?

Psychics and mediums are frequently asked to find missing people and objects. Some use a dowsing tool such as a pendulum to focus their impressions. You can learn how to use one yourself, especially if you had success with a divining rod (see preceding pages). If you're lucky, you may discover that you have a real gift for dowsing.

So how do you get a pendulum? It's easy; you can make one yourself—it's simply a weighted object suspended on a length of thread, string, or a thin metal chain. You can use almost anything: some people prefer objects they wear all the time such as a plain wedding band suspended from a favorite gold chain. You could even use a small metal key. If you're buying a pendulum, there are beautifully carved wooden examples, or you might be attracted to a shaped crystal. Choose what feels right for you.

Once you've got your pendulum, put your own energy vibrations into it; handle it frequently and keep it with you constantly. You can "charge" it with healing energy and use it to detect health problems by dowsing your own or someone else's body. Explore what's happening by asking the pendulum detailed questions, then "beam" healing energy from it onto the affected spot.

You also can use the pendulum to locate and heal disturbed spirits or negative energies in sites and buildings that have a troubled spiritual atmosphere.

Insider info DOWSING

It is a great tool for helping you to choose things— *from recommended courses to remedies of different types. You will need pictorial representations of your choices. If, for example, you want to know whether you'd find it more beneficial to take a scuba diving or sewing course, put your finger on the image of each in turn and ask the pendulum if this one will be helpful to you.*

Using it with a map can help you locate something or someone. *Position the pendulum over a map and see whether it is more active over a particular area. This may be where to find missing persons, or ancient sacred sites, hidden caves, water, or mineral deposits.*

It also can be used to identify problems. *If you feel you may have a food allergy, line up some possible suspects such as dairy or wheat foods and dip a finger into each in turn. Ask your pendulum if this particular food is bad for you. Keep checking right through the list—there may be more than one food that is causing a problem.*

HOW TO PROGRAM YOUR PENDULUM

1 *You need to program positive/negative responses into your pendulum. To do this, hold its cord between your thumb and fingertip and suspend the pendulum over a flat surface. Wait until it is completely still.*

2 *Gently swing the pendulum diagonally in front of you; concentrate your thoughts and say out loud: "This is yes." Repeat this several times.*

3 *Now swing it gently in the opposite direction and say: "This is no." Again, do this repeatedly.*

4 *Now check the pendulum for accuracy. Say your name out loud and ask it: "Is this my name?" It should react with a "yes" response. Then say a completely different name and ask the same question again. This time you should get a "no" reply.*

HOW TO FIND LOST OBJECTS

1 *If you've lost something, your pendulum can help to find it. First check out the general location—ask the pendulum a series of questions to confirm whether the lost object is in the office, your home, in the car, or the garden.*

2 *Once you've got a positive answer, be more specific. If the object is somewhere in your home, ask which room it is in. Is it in the bedroom, bathroom, or kitchen?*

3 *When you've got a "yes" answer to one of these questions, take your pendulum to the specified room and turn around slowly, asking the pendulum which direction to follow. It should point you straight there.*

Who's Got Your Number?

How can your name have a hidden meaning? And in what way does it define your essential character and destiny? The answer is the powerful link between letters and numbers. The ancient Egyptians attributed magic numbers to particular letters and used them to foretell the future. But the science of numbers (numerology) originated in Greek and Hebrew cultures. The Hebraic system known as the Cabbala attributed a specific number to each of the 22 letters of the Hebrew alphabet. So any word can be reduced to an arithmetical figure, and holds a secret meaning.

This explains why the original name your parents chose for you is so significant. It was created by the natural laws of universal attraction at your birth, and is more important than any other name you'll acquire, including your married surname.

When you discover your personal numbers of destiny (below) and explore their meanings (see opposite) you may discover surprising new insights into your character.

Your birthdate produces your life number, which is fixed and unchanging and represents your special characteristics and attributes and innermost nature. Your name number is the way you express yourself outwardly, your personality. Your two numbers can work in harmony or be antithetical. In the latter case, this may explain why you feel that deep-seated needs that you have are not being expressed.

PRIMARY VIBRATIONS

Here's how you can calculate your two personal numbers of destiny.

1	2	3	4	5	6	7	8	9
A	B	C	D	E	F	G	H	I
J	K	L	M	N	O	P	Q	R
S	T	U	V	W	X	Y	Z	

The first number is based on your date of birth

1 *To formulate this, write out your full birth date: for instance,* **December 2, 1958** *becomes* **12/2/1958**.

2 *Now add up each number:*

1 + 2 + 2 + 1 + 9 + 5 + 8 = 28;

then add both final digits to achieve a single figure:

2 + 8 = 10, *which reduces to a final figure of* **1**.

So: **12/2/1958 = 1**

THE NUMBERS AND THEIR MEANINGS

Remember, each number has its positive and negative aspects—how you use them is up to you.

1 *Independent, self-reliant, tenacious, single-minded. Intolerant, conceited, narrow, stubborn.*

2 *Placid, just, unselfish, harmonious, sociable. Irresolute, indifferent, unable to take responsibility, weak-willed.*

3 *Freedom-seeking, brave, adventurous, exuberant, brilliant. Indifferent, impatient, over-confident, lacking in stamina.*

4 *Stolid, loyal, imperturbable, honest, strong-willed, practical. Clumsy, dull, conservative, inflexible.*

5 *Adventurous, vivacious, courageous, healthy, sympathetic. Rash, irresponsible, inconstant, unreliable, thoughtless.*

6 *Idealistic, selfless, honest, charitable, faithful, responsible. Superior, weak, impractical, submissive.*

7 *Wise, discerning, philosophical, enduring, deep, contemplative. Morbid, hypercritical, inactive, antisocial.*

8 *Practical, powerful, business-like, decisive, controlling, constant. Unimaginative, blunt, self-sufficient.*

9 *Intelligent, understanding, discreet, artistic, brilliant, lofty. Dreamy, lethargic, lacking in concentration, aimless.*

Note: traditionally the numbers 11 and 22 should not be broken down to single figures.

11 *This is the number of the super intellect or genius, also regarded as a lucky person. Transformation.*

22 *Because of its great power this number may result in outstanding ascendancy or disastrous downfall.*

The next significant formula is the one derived from analyzing your given name

3 *To reduce your name to a final figure, check the graph opposite for the number corresponding to your name.*

My first name is:
J = 1 U = 3 L = 3 I = 9 E = 5

This adds up to **21***; broken down to single figures* **2 + 1 = 3**

My family name is:
S = 1 O = 6 S = 1 K = 2 I = 9 N = 5

This adds up to **24***; then, broken down to single figures* **2 + 4 = 6**

So, added together, both my names, Julie and Soskin total **9***.*

4 *Your birthday and name numbers are unique to you— check their meanings from the list above.*

PSYCHIC HEALING

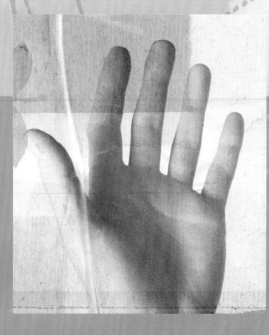

4

What are Your Healing Powers?

Did you know that you unknowingly implement some form of healing every day? You give a stranger a smile, take time to listen to a colleague, send out a kindly thought to a far-away relative, feel compassion for someone you read about, and call a friend when you sense that he or she is feeling sad. When you've hurt your own hand, you instinctively rub it to make it feel better. Whenever you make these ordinary expressions of love and concern, you are sending out healing energies.

Distant Healing

You can make these actions even more effective by learning how to enhance your natural healing energies. This may take the form of distant healing, whereby you "send" powerful, beneficial thoughts to someone in need. For example, when I was very young I joined a psychic development group. We were asked to think of someone who would benefit from absent healing. A friend was going through a difficult emotional patch, so I put her name into the healing energy. I went to visit her the following Sunday; she told us that on the previous Thursday evening she had suddenly experienced a powerful wave of feeling sweeping over her. She also had been swept by a reassuring sense that everything would be fine. This had happened around 7:45pm, the time when our group had met and held the healing session. My friend had no idea about my psychic interests and certainly didn't know about the group.

Guidelines for psychic healing

If you find that you're a "natural" healer, it can be flattering to your ego—but don't get carried away.

Know that any "hands-on" work you do is one part of a much wider healing process. You are simply a channel for healing energies. Healing energy (often called prana) comes from a universal source, not from you.

Remember you are the instrument or channel for healing energy, therefore self-awareness and spiritual development will greatly assist you.

Don't diagnose or play doctor and never contradict medical advice given by a professional to another person.

A Channel for Healing

You also can work on getting in touch with your inner sources of regenerative energy (see opposite page) and use this to promote well-being in others. Although all people have the ability to promote healing, some can do so more directly (see box on opposite page). If you "test" empathetic, for example, people may begin to feel better just by being near you. If you are shamanistic, you should have an innate sense of what will harm or help someone who is ill. If you have true psychic healing ability, others will benefit directly from your healing touch. If your healing ability appears more spiritual, then you may serve as a channeler for healing by higher powers.

FINDING THE POWER WITHIN

In order for yourself or others to gain positive benefit, learn to access your inner sources of regenerative energy.

1 *Sit in a relaxed position and place both hands onto your solar plexus.*

2 *Close your eyes and focus your entire awareness onto your hands. Gradually they will become warmer from the prana energy stored in your solar plexus.*

3 *Now place your fingers very gently onto your forehead. This will make them tingle and feel alive with energy.*

4 *Let the streams of prana energy flow into your head; notice the vivid sensations this causes.*

5 *When the tingling stops, take your fingers away and shake your hands energetically for a few moments.*

6 *Finally, return your hands to your solar plexus. Let them rest there for a few moments. They should now feel alive and "glowing" with energy.*

What kind of healer are you?

❑ **1** Are you a good listener?

❑ **2** Do you make others feel at ease?

❑ **3** Can you feel a connection with the earth and nature?

❑ **4** Do people confide in you?

❑ **5** Can you "shake off" a headache?

❑ **6** Do you want to make the world a better place?

❑ **7** Have you ever felt the presence of an angelic or healing guide?

❑ **8** Do you have an intuitive link with animals?

❑ **9** Do you often feel completely at one with the world?

❑ **10** Do you feel other people's pain?

❑ **11** After you've visited or phoned, do your friends feel better?

❑ **12** Could you "decide" not to be unwell?

If you answered yes to

1 2 4
You are empathetic.

3 8 10
You're shamanistic.

5 11 12
Your gift is psychic healing.

6 7 9
You have spiritual healing ability.

(See opposite page)

Healing Yourself First

If you discover that you have an effective healing ability, it's only natural to feel proud of yourself. But you also would be getting the wrong message. Always remember that the only *personal* healing skill that you can honestly claim is the ability to heal yourself. In all other instances, you merely act as a channel for life-force energy or prana. That is what promotes healing in others.

Once you have understood this, you'll also realize that, in order to become an effective healer, you will need to sort out your own health first. This means resolving both emotional and physical problems—healing yourself demands great self-awareness and acceptance. It also means giving up any long-held grudges, resentments, and other negative feelings, however justified they may have seemed until now.

You shouldn't be too hard on yourself, though; never underestimate how much self-healing you can achieve simply by not thinking too much about the past or the future. Live and enjoy your life as it is today: you're the sum total of all your experiences and whatever is left unresolved from your past will manifest itself in the here and now. Observe, acknowledge, and confront what is in your life, and you'll activate a vibrant, flowing, energy through which you can prosper and grow.

Natural Powers

The exercises on the opposite page are designed to help you emulate and access the abilities of other common creatures. Butterfly breathing is all about becoming "powerful" quickly—just as the butterfly gains its beauty and final form in short order, while we all recognize the short, sharp sting of the bee.

Insider info HEALING OR PRANA ENERGY

Healing energy is present inside all of us. *People are born with this prana energy and it links you with everything in the universe—all forms of matter, both animate and inanimate.*

The stores of this energy can be increased. *You can boost your levels of prana by linking with universal energy during meditation (see page 23), by making positive affirmations (see page 34), and by balancing your chakras (see page 31).*

There are special sources of this energy. *Prana flows through everything, but it seems to be particularly concentrated in water and earth. Activities such as sailing, swimming, and gardening are effective and pleasurable ways of boosting your prana energy.*

BREATHE LIKE A BUTTERFLY...

Draw powerful healing forces quickly into your body along with your breath.

1 *Place your hands on your heart and take a really deep breath. As you do this, push your arms and hands up straight toward the sky. Mentally link yourself with the boundless sources of prana or universal energy.*

2 *As you breathe out, let your arms and hands fall to your sides.*

3 *Repeat this up to ten times, drawing increasing amounts of prana energy into and around your body.*

...STING LIKE A BEE

Use your powers of visualization to zap cold and flu viruses, and other enemies of your immune system.

1 *Make yourself completely relaxed (see page 23) and mentally scan your entire body from top to toe, sensing any areas of your body that are affected.*

2 *Focus your concentration onto these areas and visualize armies of strong "soldier" cells marching out to search and destroy the invasive virus.*

3 *Be as graphic and detailed with your imagery as possible—give your soldier cells incredibly powerful weapons to make them truly effective.*

4 *Watch your "troops" destroying the virus—the more imaginative energy you put into this the better it will work.*

Healing Your Garden

Many psychic healers have flourishing, healthy plants in their gardens. This is not at all surprising: energy directed into plants through benign human contact can makes a dramatic difference to their health. Experiments have shown that plants that are regularly touched and stroked do noticeably better than their neglected companions. These discoveries by plant researchers make complete sense to a practicing psychic—loving communication automatically promotes healing and well-being, and positive focus onto the aura of living things can produce highly beneficial outcomes.

Each plant has its unique spirit counterpart—you often see them illustrated as fairies, gnomes, or pixies. It is no coincidence that people put statues of these in their gardens—they are instinctively acknowledging the hidden world of the earth spirits and unconsciously asking them to help.

If you want to make your plants blissfully healthy and happy, focus your psychic energies on your gardening skills. For a start, you should learn to communicate with the spirits of the plants in your garden (see page 58). By doing so, you will enable them to grow stronger and live longer.

THREE-STEP RESCUE REMEDY

Even if a plant seems to be on its last legs, you can give it a chance to flourish.

1 *If parts of the plant are already dead, remove these and clear the soil around it. Now connect with the plant and ask it what's wrong? Is it is too dry, waterlogged, or in the wrong soil? Trust your intuition.*

2 *Correct any imbalances you've sensed—repotting the plant may be necessary if the soil is unsuitable—then focus healing energy into the plant, from the roots upward.*

3 *Visualize a bright life-line of energy going from you, down into the plant's roots, up through its leaves and back to you again in a continuous cycle. Do this until you intuitively feel that the plant has absorbed enough healing.*

TOP TIPS FOR PSYCHIC GARDENING

Make your garden grow beautifully by using all your psychic skills. Project nourishment into the soil, discourage pests, draw in nature's helpers, and generate positive energy for your plants.

Nourishment *Enriched soil means healthy plants: feed it with homemade organic compost (a good gardening book will tell you how to make it). As you dig in the compost, visualize your garden full of glossy-leaved flourishing plants.*

Water *Many psychic gardeners like to "power" water before using it on their plants. Pour it alternately from one container to another to infuse it with prana or life energy, or use a crystal (see page 112) to beam healing energy into it.*

Pest protection *Offer a sacrifice to slugs, snails, and bugs. For instance, you can make a bargain with the spirits of snails. Agree that they can have a certain number of your fruit and vegetables, leaving the rest free for your own use.*

Helpful creatures *Give a warm welcome to useful creatures such as ladybugs and frogs by invoking their aid. They will keep down destructive pests and help you to maintain your garden in a dynamic, healthy balance.*

Mood *Make everything in your garden feel loved and appreciated by walking around regularly and checking that all is well. If you choose a special place in the garden for your meditation, the positive energies will be greatly enhanced.*

Healing with Crystals

If you've ever had a strong attraction to a crystal or gemstone, don't ignore that feeling. You may have found an ideal psychic healing partner. Each stone carries the energy of its time spent deep in the earth; it not only acts as a powerful focus for healing work, but will actively enhance the process.

There are many kinds of crystals available in specialist mineral, new age, or museum shops, and it's easy to feel overwhelmed by so much choice. For practical purposes, however, an effective psychic healer needs just one gemstone, programmed and dedicated for this particular task. A piece of clear, unblemished rock quartz with one, well-defined, pointed end, is excellent for most healing work; choose one that fits comfortably in your hand. Alternatively, raw amethyst is another wonderfully effective healing stone.

Once you've chosen your crystal, you can prepare it for healing work by linking it up with your own energy (see right). Your crystal is then ready for action; to implement healing, use the simple but effective technique described on the page opposite. This restores energy levels that have been sapped by pain and illness; at the same time, it triggers the healing resources that are already present in the person you're helping.

Whatever crystal you choose, take good care of your stone and keep it in a safe place. You should cleanse it regularly (see right) to remove any negative energy it may have absorbed.

Cleansing guidelines

Crystals retain and magnify energy more than any other material, so regular cleansing is crucial. Here are a few simple methods:

Hold the crystal for a few minutes under clear, running water.

Place the crystal on a clean, non-plastic plate (china is best) and put it in direct sunlight for at least a couple of hours.

Visualize a ray of clear, bright light thoroughly cleansing the stone.

POWERING YOUR CRYSTAL

Before using your crystal for healing work, you need to activate its latent energies.

1 Wash your crystal under clear running water for a few moments. Dry it, then keep it close to your body for a few days to align its vibrations as closely as possible with your own. You might like to keep it under your pillow at night while you're asleep.

2 When you're ready to charge the crystal, sit in a quiet place and relax completely, holding it gently in your hands. Focus your concentration onto the crystal.

3 Look deep into the crystal; at the same time, invoking the highest good or other spiritual guardian, mentally direct a sustained pulse of healing energy into the crystal, from the base to its apex.

4 You'll feel the crystal "throbbing" in your hand; when you sense that it is fully programmed, wrap it in a clean piece of white cotton or linen and store it in a safe place.

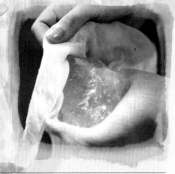

HEALING WITH A CRYSTAL

This method is excellent for general healing work—it is both safe and effective.

1 Make sure that the person who is receiving healing is comfortable and relaxed—he or she may prefer to lie down, or lean back in a reclining chair—and that the room is calm and quiet.

2 Take your crystal in your right hand, and mentally link with its vibrations until you feel a "throbbing" sensation in your hand.

3 Angle the point of the crystal at a spot about 12 inches over the head of the person you're treating, and slowly move the crystal clockwise around his or her body. As you do this, visualize a "laser" beam of energy pulsing from your crystal. Repeat this

several times until you have completely surrounded the person's body with a healing force field.

4 If you sense that an area needs specific healing, direct the crystal's pointed end at that site for a few moments. Target energy onto it until you feel ready to move on.

5 You will know instinctively when you have done enough. At this point, transfer the crystal into your left hand, and visualize the crystal's energy flowing gently back into itself. There are no guarantees of success, as with all healing, but practice will increase your abilities.

Once you're confident about using a crystal for healing, you may want to extend your range, and explore other kinds of gemstones. Again, these are widely available from specialist mineral and museum shops or by mail order. Most new-age magazines contain advertisements from gemstone suppliers.

If you feel attracted to gemstone healing, you'll find it leads you to the chakra centers of the body. These actively respond to the vibrations from different gemstones, and, if you choose the right ones, you can use them to energize and heal, as described on the page opposite. The chakras play a key part in every aspect of your well-being—physical, mental and spiritual—and have a direct influence on the health of your aura. Each chakra has its own signature color, so it's important to choose the right stone for healing at these centers. When choosing your chakra crystals, let your intuition guide you, and spend time exploring, touching, sensing, and assessing the vibrations from all the different kinds on display. At some point, one stone will feel just right. You'll know this by instinct—it is almost as if it is saying: "Choose me!"

The Crown Center

A suitable gem for this center could be a piece of clear quartz, a deep violet amethyst, or a rich purple sugalite. Hold the crystal on the top of the head.

***Healing benefits** Calms feelings of constant anxiety, insecurity, and alienation from others.*

The Throat Center

Choose from blue gems such as sapphire, turquoise, lapis lazuli, aquamarine and blue lace agate. Cradle the crystal in the hollow of the throat.

***Healing benefits** Sore throats, coughs, and swollen glands can all be eased.*

The Solar Plexus Center

Go for golden gems such as citrine, amber, yellow topaz, and citrine, and place the crystal you chose just above the navel.

***Healing benefits** Helps with food disorders such as anorexia and bulimia; and calms any stress centered in the gut.*

The Base Center

Choose the earthy colors of red jasper, or a red-brown tiger's eye. You can also use a plain black pebble. Rest your chosen crystal at the base of the spine.

***Healing benefits** Use for aching bones, stress, and irritable bowel syndrome.*

The Brow Center

The deep indigo shade of sodalite works well on this chakra. Balance the crystal on the spot between the eyes.

Healing benefits *Good for "fuzzy" headaches, blurred vision, disturbed sleep, and general nervousness.*

The Heart Center

Look for green gems such as malachite, moss agate, or jade. Alternatively, you can use a pink stone such as rose quartz or rhodonite. Position your crystal at the center of the chest area.

Healing benefits *Alleviates bronchitis, asthma, chest infections, heart problems, and violent emotional reactions.*

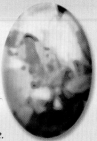

The Sacral Center

Use stimulating orange from colored gems such as amber, carnelian, orange agate and orange pebbles. Put the crystal on the genital area.

Healing benefits *Good for problems with menstruation, PMT, infertility, and impotence.*

Using Sound to Heal

A mother cradles her child, singing a familiar lullaby, and murmurs soothing, loving words. The baby has already become attuned to her voice in the womb, and responds with cooing, gurgling sounds, completing the loop of intimate harmony. This ordinary event is just one aspect of the power of sound.

This force has been known from the dawn of time: "In the beginning was the Word." This single phrase from the Bible (St John 1:1) signifies the release of an astounding energy, through which the entire world was created.

Music, too, has profound psychic power; some traditions hold that every musical note represents a spirit being. The Indian musician Ravi Shankar believes that sound is God; and he regards music as a spiritual path, leading to divine peace and bliss.

When you psychically attune yourself to sound, you can direct its healing forces inside yourself. Using music for meditation can help restore and revive yourself in mind, while stimulating your chakras with sound can help to correct any imbalances that are causing ill-health or disease.

THE HEART OF MUSIC

Meet the healing spirits in music through this simple meditation.

1 *Choose a piece of music that always makes you peaceful and reflective, and play it as you enter a calm, meditative state (see page 23). Now focus on the music, and let it take you to the highest spiritual level.*

2 *As you go deeper into meditation and contemplation, feel yourself completely united with the cosmos.*

3 *Let the sound of the music play into your consciousness, so that it becomes part of your own rhythm. Attune your entire being to the dance of the song, and now connect with the spirits within the music.*

4 *At this point, ask the spirits of the music to bring you healing, and open yourself to them. Do this until you feel restored and revived, then return to your normal state.*

SING TO YOUR CHAKRAS

1 *Concentrate on your breath as shown on page 23, then close your eyes. Visualize the red, spinning disk of your base chakra, focusing at its center. Listen attentively. You will hear the sonic pitch of the chakra intuitively (the lower centers have deep notes, which become higher as you progress up the body).*

2 *Sing out the note you hear, pitching its sound to the exact vibration you feel at the base chakra. This is a strong note, with the sound "OO."*

3 *Next, focus on the orange disk of the sacral chakra; tune into its sound vibration as before, then sing out its note to the sound "OR."*

4 *Now imagine the brilliant yellow core of the solar plexus chakra; listen for its special note, then sing it out to the sound "AH."*

5 *Move on to the green center of the heart chakra next; wait for its note, then sing it as the open sound "ARE."*

6 *Next, focus onto the clear sky blue of the throat chakra. Tune into its note, and sing it as a short clipped "A" sound (as in apple).*

7 *Conjure up the deep indigo depths of the brow chakra; focus onto its sonic pitch, and sing it to the sound 'E' (as in even).*

8 *Now visualize the pure violet color of your crown chakra. Listen intently until you hear its note, then sing it to the sound "E-OO."*

9 *Finally, focus your concentration back to the heart center, and hum softly to yourself until you feel completely in tune throughout your body.*

Healing Yourself with Color

Did you know that color is so powerful, it can influence your breathing rhythms? Exposure to a red light alerts your mind, raises your blood pressure, arouses your emotions, and spurs you into action. Conversely, all these reactions will be reversed by using the calming effect of blue.

You can use the therapeutic power of color in various ways—but the best place to start is in your own home. Whether you have a tiny apartment or a spacious family dwelling, a sensitive choice of color can transform your living environment into a positive healing zone.

When you're planning to decorate a space in your home, consult the chart (right) to see what psychic impact each color makes. To help you to sleep better, for example, you could bring the calming action of soft green to your bedroom. Conversely, the bright, joyful energy of red is best for action spots such as children's play rooms, while inspiring sunshine yellow is perfect for a study or work room.

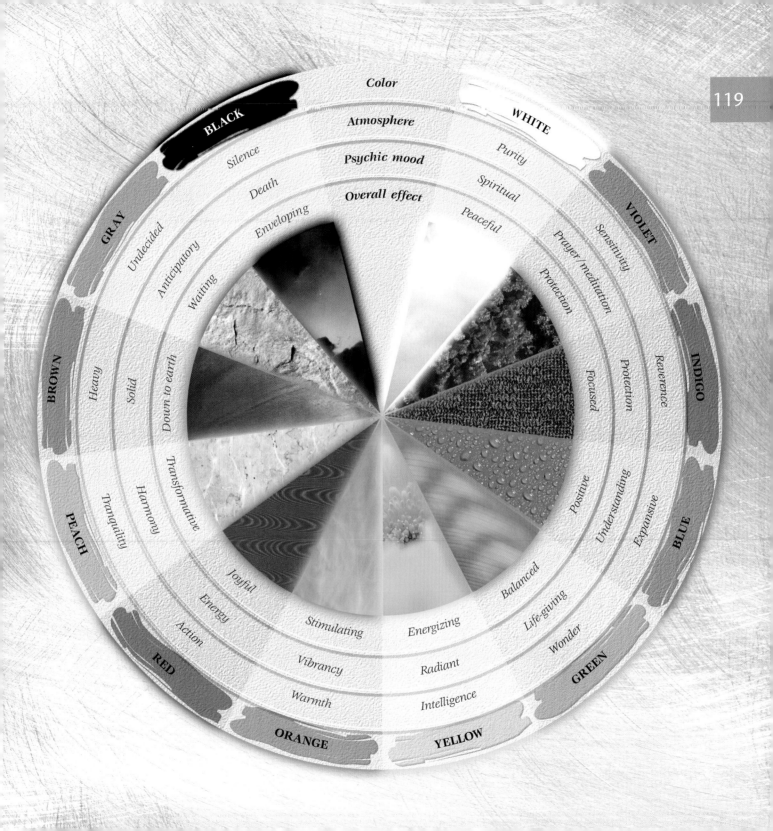

Color

Atmosphere

Psychic mood

Overall effect

BLACK

WHITE

Silence

Purity

Death

Spiritual

GRAY

VIOLET

Enveloping

Peaceful

Undecided

Sensitivity

Anticipatory

Prayer/meditation

Waiting

Protection

BROWN

INDIGO

Heavy

Protection

Solid

Focused

Down to earth

Reverence

Transformative

Positive

Understanding

PEACH

Expansive

Tranquility

BLUE

Harmony

Balanced

Joyful

Life-giving

Energy

Wonder

Action

GREEN

RED

Stimulating

Vibrancy

Energizing

Warmth

Radiant

ORANGE

Intelligence

YELLOW

Color energy is already active at the very core of your being, at the "grass roots" of your chakra centers. The best way to keep yourself in peak mental, emotional, and spiritual balance is to breathe color into your chakras as described on page 31. Do this exercise regularly, using the color pages that follow on pages 122–37, and you'll also maintain a balanced, healthy aura.

However, at certain times you may want to use color in a more direct way, to target specific problems. For instance, you can enclose yourself in a circle of therapeutic color (right), or channel colored light into your body, as shown opposite. Each color has particular healing properties, and these techniques help you to "zero in" on a range of ailments, such as arthritis, raised blood pressure, nervous exhaustion, and anxiety.

HOW COLORS HEAL

The time each color needs to take effect varies. Follow these guidelines, and don't exceed the recommended times.

Red 7 minutes	Orange 10 minutes	Yellow 12 minutes
Energizes, improves circulation, raises blood pressure. Use for sciatica. Do not use it if you suffer from hypertension.	*Helps digestion and improves your metabolism. Good for rheumatism, cramps, spasms, and asthma.*	*Stimulates the nervous system, liver, pancreas and kidneys. Use it to treat constipation and arthritis.*

A HEALING CIRCLE OF COLOR

Surround yourself with therapeutic color to relieve a health problem.

1 Read the list of colors and their healing properties (below), and choose the one best suited to your problem. If you're feeling stressed, for instance, green may help.

2 Lie down comfortably, with your arms at your sides, and use the breathing exercise on page 23 to relax completely.

3 Visualize yourself enclosed in a glowing circle of your chosen color, and focus on your heart center. Breathe the color into this center and visualize it circulating throughout your aura for a few minutes.

4 If you find this gives relief, increase the time spent circulating the color—10–20 minutes should be enough.

RADIANT COLOR THERAPY

Use colored light to beam healing energy into your body.

1 Check the list of colors for their healing action (below), and choose the one you need. If you have digestive trouble, for example, orange can help.

2 Fix an appropriately colored light bulb into an adjustable desk lamp or tape a translucent sheet of the appropriately colored paper across the bottom of the shade. Put the lamp on the floor and switch it on.

3 Take off your shoes and socks, and sit on the floor with your legs out straight. Your feet should be about 18 inches away from the lamp. Direct the light beam onto the center of the sole of one foot—this is a natural route for color energy to flow into your body.

4 For balanced healing, treat both feet; check the colors (below) for advice on how much time you need.

Green 15 minutes	Turquoise 15 minutes	Blue 15 minutes	Violet 15 minutes
Brings mental and physical equilibrium, and is excellent for stress. Use as directed to avoid over-stimulating the heart.	Refreshing and restful, it strengthens both the immune and nervous systems. Soothes inflammation and eczema.	An excellent all-purpose healing color. Reduces blood pressure, and promotes the healthy growth of cells and body tissue.	Improves mental stability, helps to purify the body and raises self-esteem. It is also excellent to treat shock.

Dynamic Red

The warm, life-affirming potency of red influences you at primal levels. Its energy courses through your body in your blood, and also activates your Base chakra, the psychic center that links to the inner core of the planet. Deep within the earth is where a fierce, glowing energy can be found—and this is what gives you your basic appetite for life. This is why red lifts your spirits and stimulates your blood; it also can generate great emotional intensity, ranging from a fierce protectiveness, passion and aggression to sudden violence.

Shades of Red

You can absorb red in its brightest, purest form but its color differs depending on what is happening to you. Your aura will reflect this: a light red shows your spontaneous, playful side, while deep, rich shades indicate courage, endurance, and strong emotions. If the color is noticeably dark or muddy, however, this signals dangerously blocked, frustrated energy.

Restoring the Balance

An imbalance of red in your system is reflected not only in your aura but you may be "red in the face" with frustration or anger. Should you suffer a shock, defeat, or trauma, your core reserves of life energy will be seriously depleted. Correct these extremes by using the chakra balancing exercise described on page 31. Visualize your Base chakra glowing with a pure red energy—and use the image on the facing page for inspiration.

Healing with Red

Psychic healers use red to boost blood circulation, stimulate energy, and to ease aching joints and muscles. If stress has severely overtaxed your adrenal glands, so that you're completely exhausted and run down, red can bring you back to life again.

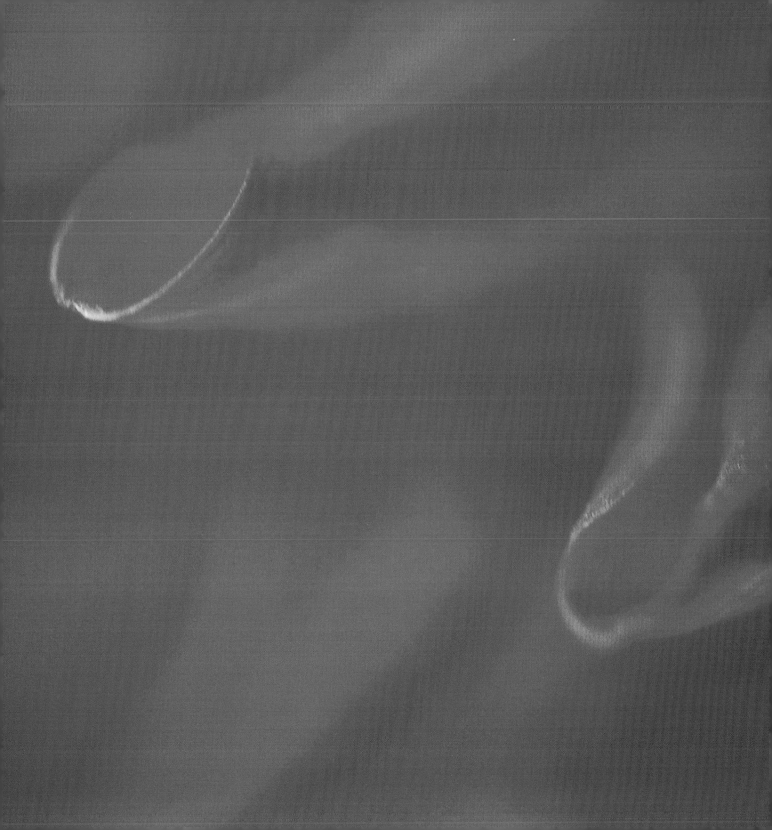

Joyful Orange

The warming glow at the heart of a flame is the perfect representation of orange's cheerful energy. This is what activates your Sacral chakra, and is expressed in joyful, instinctive, love of life. Orange energy stimulates your pleasure in food, music, dance, and sex, while nourishing a deep sense of well-being, happiness, and abundance.

Shades of Orange

A pure, clear orange in your aura is a positive sign of energy, optimism, imagination, focus, and purpose, but various shades may appear, depending on what is going on in your life. For instance, a light, orange-yellow tint indicates highly creative mental activity, while at the opposite end of the scale, a reddish-orange can reflect confusion, ambivalence, cunning and repressed emotions. A very dark or muddy shade warns of uncontrolled self-indulgence.

Restoring the Balance

If orange is severely out of balance in your system, this will be reflected in the shades of the color in your aura, but it will show in your external behavior also. Too much and you're never satisfied, seeking endless gratification from food, possessions, sex, or money. Too little, and your joy in life may have been depleted by extreme deprivation of some kind, and this may result in lack of vitality and depression. To restore your aura to health, balance your chakras as shown on page 31—and use the image on the facing page to inspire you.

Healing with Orange

Orange is a superb tonic for the reproductive system and it recharges your batteries when you are tired, stressed, or ill. In the right proportions, it also acts as a natural corrective agent, enabling you to know when "enough is enough," and restoring you to health and vitality.

Illuminating Yellow

The signature color of the Solar Plexus chakra—the center that generates your sense of personal power, self-worth, and achievement—yellow is also the color of the sun, with its positive qualities of radiance, openness, clarity, and warmth. The power of yellow in your life is twofold: on the physical level it enables you to be comfortable with yourself; intellectually, it promotes clear thinking, open communication, analysis, logic, judgment, and intelligence. Yellow can give you the supreme self-confidence to realize your ideas, but it may also overwhelm and confuse you with too many possibilities.

Shades of Yellow

A bright, vibrant yellow in your aura reflects the sunny side of your personality. A very light yellow shade indicates areas of mystical thought, while a dull yellow points to confused, ill-defined, or unimaginative ideas. It could also reveal secretiveness and dishonesty.

Restoring the Balance

If many negative aspects of yellow are reflected in your aura, your self-esteem is probably at a low ebb. Your confidence, courage, sense of intrinsic value, and sense of humor may be lost. You can restore harmony to your system by balancing your chakras as described on page 31. Breathe the clean, clear energy of pure yellow into your Solar Plexus chakra, using the image facing this page for inspiration.

Healing with Yellow

Psychic healers use yellow to improve digestion and to eliminate toxins from the liver and gall bladder; its gently stimulating effects can also strengthen and calm an exhausted nervous system, and this helps to promote clear, effective thinking. On an emotional level, it is used to restore self-esteem and pleasure in life.

Life-giving Green

The soothing, power of green brings tranquillity and harmony to the very core of your being. It is the color energy that radiates from your Heart chakra, where it governs your ability to give and receive love, empathize with others, and find peace within yourself. Nature's own color, green brings you into a relaxed, healing contact with the world around you; but, as in nature, it can also stagnate and decay, leading to festering emotions such as jealousy and resentment.

Shades of Green

A clear, bright, green in the aura is a wholesome sign of fine judgment, adaptability, and balance, while a very light shade denotes spirituality, the ability to heal, and an intensely sympathetic nature. On the other hand, if someone is "green with envy," this would be indicated by a dark or olive green shade. A muddy or dull green points to cunning, deceit, emotional deprivation and secretiveness, a yellow-green to possessiveness, and a gray-green to depression.

Restoring the Balance

If you don't have a healthy balance of green in your aura, you may literally look "green around the gills." But however stale or sluggish you're feeling, you can use the power of pure, fresh, green to detoxify your system. Do this by balancing your chakras as described on page 31, and use the image on the facing page for inspiration while you breathe the invigorating energy of green into your Heart chakra.

Healing with Green

Green has a powerful restorative energy that regulates the heart and blood pressure, heals the lungs and chest and also removes toxins from the system. As green is the most relaxing of all colors, it soothes your frazzled nerves when you've been under pressure; it also assists the circulatory system and aids balance and harmony.

Inspirational Blue

The cool, calm, power of blue connects you with the infinite vistas of the sky and ocean, evoking spirituality, devotion and a sense of the sacred. Blue is also the color of your Throat chakra, your center of communication. When activated, this chakra inspires you to speak in the spirit of truth. Blue is an immensely far-reaching force that can be expressed through an independent personality, an aloof idealist, and, at the other extreme, a deeply emotional person who often feels overwhelmed by powerful feelings.

Shades of Blue

A clear sky-blue in your aura indicates self-confidence and mental clarity; turquoise signifies a tranquil attitude; and a soft, light hue indicates devotion to an ideal. If the blue is very pale, this points to superficial thoughts. Deeper shades may mean that you're "feeling blue" due to a phase of sadness, or a more long-term, serious depression. But some dark blues are very positive—midnight blue is a sign of enhanced intuition, while navy blue reflects a protective energy at work.

Restoring the Balance

When your system has been affected by the negative aspects of blue, your faith in life can be undermined, and you may lose perspective. You can correct these problems by doing the chakra balancing exercise described on page 31. Using the facing page, restore the effectiveness of your Throat chakra by breathing in the brilliant energy of pure blue.

Healing with Blue

Blue is an excellent pain-reliever. Psychic healers also use it to trigger the body's own healing resources—its cooling properties are useful in the treatment of thyroid, mouth and throat problems, and fever. Blue is also used to heal spiritual and emotional trauma, restoring a sense of peace and calm.

Visionary Indigo

The hypnotic, midnight blue of indigo has a transformative effect on your body and soul. It is the sign of a true mystic and is also the color of the Brow chakra. This psychic center enhances clairvoyance, and expands your psychic vision so that you are able to see past, present, and future as a unified picture. Because indigo stimulates the right side of your brain, it triggers your creative imagination, deepens your intuition, and gives you a serene, inner confidence that you know the truth. But these same qualities may also make you a remote and isolated figure, who finds it difficult to communicate with others.

Shades of Indigo

Indigo often shades into purple and violet tones in the aura, and these colors all connect you with higher levels of consciousness, promoting a wonderful sense of peace and spiritual harmony. But a pronounced level of indigo in your aura may also cause you problems. People with mystical qualities are often misunderstood, and this may result in exclusion and loneliness.

Restoring the Balance

You may be absorbed in psychic visions, but if this leads to isolation and remoteness, these are warning signs that should be heeded. By doing the chakra balancing exercise described on page 31, you can bring yourself down to earth without losing contact with your higher self. Using the image on the facing page for inspiration, integrate indigo into your entire being, and stay in touch with the joy of ordinary life.

Healing with Indigo

Indigo has a powerful sedative action, and can act as a light anesthetic. Psychic healers use it to treat mental disturbance, as it helps to clear the head. If your nerves have been frayed to the point of breakdown, indigo will come to your rescue, and restore your inner balance.

Mystical Violet

The gem-like radiance of pure violet heralds a transcendent level of consciousness, informed by the desire to know eternal truth. It signifies enlightened thought, and a profound connection with the spiritual world. Known as the color of kings, violet is worn by royalty, bishops, or popes to indicate power beyond the temporal. It is also the color of the Crown chakra, the psychic center that links you with knowledge from the deepest sources of spiritual wisdom.

Shades of Violet

When you see violet in the aura, it is usually bold and bright, and has no negative aspects. Even when the color is dark, this is not a problem—on the contrary, it signifies a near perfect connection with the divine. You may feel magnetically attracted to violet, as it has a strong psychic influence; this is fine, as long as you don't use it to fuel a fantasy of yourself as a superior spirit, in a bid to escape the demands of daily life.

Restoring the Balance

It is highly unusual to see a preponderance of violet in the aura—in fact some people have very little. This may result in a "deadened" feeling that life has no meaning beyond the purely physical. By doing the chakra balancing exercise described on page 31, you can integrate a healthy level of violet into your aura. Using the image on the facing page for inspiration, breathe violet into your Crown center, to help you stay in harmonious contact with your higher self.

Healing with Violet

Violet calms the brain and nervous system and helps dispel irrational obsessions and neuroses. It is used by psychic healers to treat shock trauma, or emotional distubance. Violet has a cooling effect on rashes and sunburn, the pineal gland, and the eyes, and balances your metabolism. It is used also to provide effective psychic protection.

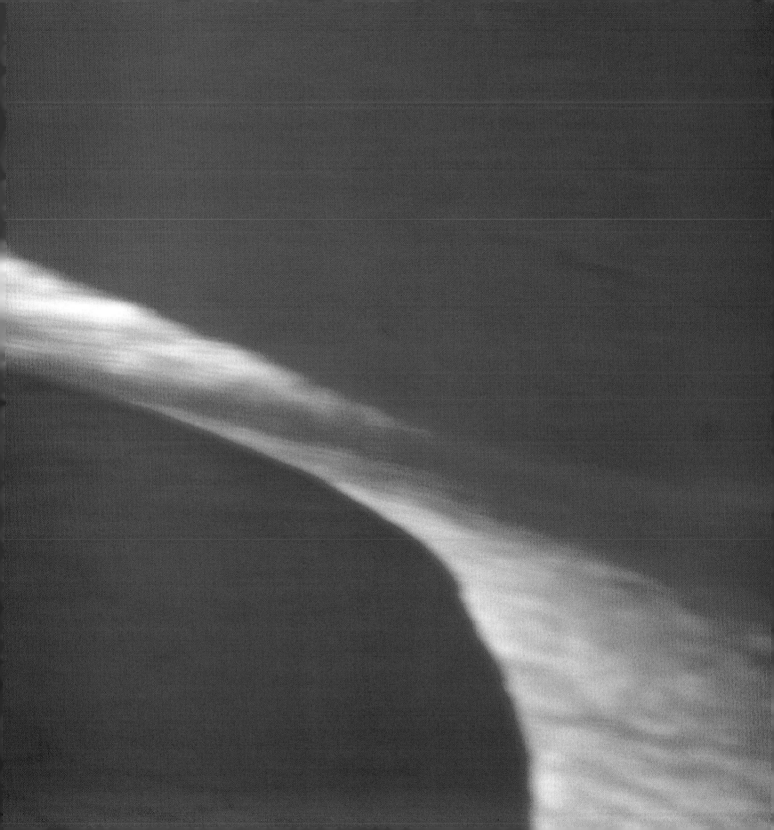

Purifying White

The quiet grace of newly fallen snow is the perfect image of both the beauty and silence of white, the color that represents the fully awakened spirit. Its pure, clean, energy expands your mind into a luminous stream of white light, connecting you to the highest levels of consciousness through your Crown chakra. This experience brings profound spiritual relief and release, and an immensely peaceful sense of distance from all emotional confusion and mental clutter.

Shades of White

White is very rarely seen in the aura, as it signifies a fully enlightened being. If white *is* present, it will usually emanate from the crown of the head, and is a sign that the person is receiving inspiration from a high spiritual source. When this happens, pure light is drawn in from the cosmos and filters throughout the aura, enhancing its radiance.

Restoring the Balance

Connecting with white is a perfect way to cleanse yourself in mind, body, and spirit. Focus your breathing as described on page 31, then imaginatively link yourself with the highest source of spiritual energy. Using the picture opposite for inspiration, visualize white light flowing into your Crown center, and traveling through all your chakras in a shining beam of energy. With each breath, expand this white light into every part of your aura. Finally, seal the energy within yourself by visualizing a band of gold around your entire aura.

Healing with White

When you are in complete despair, white can exert a powerful, healing, force. It purifies your thoughts, promotes calm reflection, and helps to restore you to a wider, healthier, spiritual perspective. This means that you can accept events that you cannot control, and have faith that they can't destroy your spirit.

ENCOUNTERING SPIRITS

5

Could You be a Shaman?

Great healers and clairvoyants, shamans are found in many cultures, including Native American and Australian aboriginal groups. Most shamans pass through a gateway to the "other world" of spirits. Here, they can talk to their ancestors and get help from them. Shamans enter a sacred space where they go into a trance, meditate, and plug directly into the planet's energy.

If you have an unusually close affinity with plants and animals, you may feel a natural empathy with shamanism. Being close to the natural world can make you better able to help the people close to you. You'll "know" what's good for them and what's bad. You can strengthen this bond with nature by making regular links with plant spirits as shown on page 58. You also can create your own version of a sacred space (see below). Going inside this sanctuary may be your first experience of meeting your "real" self, with a new sense of connection with the world around you. Shamanism is as much about drawing on the reservoir of ancient wisdom as it is about reaching out to help others.

A SACRED SPACE

To experience what it's like being a shaman, create your own sacred space. From this "home base" you can contact the essence of your secret inner world, using all your senses.

1 *Focus on your breathing as described on page 23. Invoke the image of an outdoor space where you feel completely secure and at peace with yourself—it could be a beach, a woodland, a river bank, or a favorite spot in your garden.*

2 *As you meditate, visualize yourself right there in your safe place. Feel the ground beneath your feet, and sense the air around you. Open all your senses and explore the landscape—there may be trees, flowers, sand, rocks, glittering sea spray, or a river flowing between grassy banks.*

3 *Take time to absorb the spirit of this unique place, letting its atmosphere soak through your skin.*

4 *Using your breath as a focus, breathe in and hold the picture steady. Then, on the out breath, let the picture grow in intensity and movement, and watch as mists form and billow.*

5 *When you feel completely at one with this vision, hold the image, then allow yourself to dissolve into the mist. When you're ready, return to your everyday world.*

6 *Repeat this connection frequently until it becomes as easy as stepping outside your own front door. In time, your sacred place will develop a life of its own—you'll be able to watch flowers and trees growing, and see all the natural cycles of life taking place.*

THE SPIRAL PATH

*A shaman has to walk the "Spiral Path," a psychic
initiation that gives insight into the mysteries of the inner
and outer worlds. Labyrinth walking can be done in a
similar spirit in order to gain personal knowledge.*

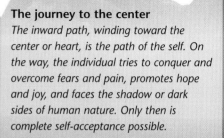

The journey to the center
*The inward path, winding toward the
center or heart, is the path of the self. On
the way, the individual tries to conquer and
overcome fears and pain, promotes hope
and joy, and faces the shadow or dark
sides of human nature. Only then is
complete self-acceptance possible.*

Going to the outer edge
*The corresponding path leads outward into
the world. This is where the shaman or
individual gets in touch with the planet.
The goal is to meet the secret spirits in all
living things, and see the entire "web of
being" linked by a stream of endless
energy.*

Complete union
*If you complete this psychic journey, you
probably would have met dark aspects of
the self and possibly encountered strange
spirit creatures. The reward for completing
this psychic journey is the experience of
"falling into wonder"—a unity with the
endless, vibrating energies of the universe.*

Contact with Departed Spirits

When you're fully absorbed in your daily life, you may not have much time and space to think deeply about other levels of existence. But all that can change when someone close to you dies; this is the moment when you may start to wonder what happens to the human spirit after death. Most psychics believe that the souls of people who have died enter the astral or spirit worlds. You may already have visited these realms during an astral dream, or when astral traveling (see page 72), and met the spirit of someone you've loved. Some people also claim to do so during "near death" experiences.

A visit to the spirit world is not always a one-way journey—a departed spirit may decide to come and visit you. In fact, some psychics believe that it is not possible to "command" the spirit of a person to return against his or her will, it is the spirit who decides to make contact with you. Many people report experiencing visits from loved ones shortly after their deaths. If this happens, you might simply accept it as a natural event, without feeling the need to explore the matter further.

On the other hand, it may make you very curious about what happens after death—you may even feel

Insider info MEDIUMS

The role of a medium *is to contact the spirits of people who have died and are now in the astral or spirit world. The medium usually does this on behalf of people who have lost someone close to them.*

Contact between loved ones *can be very comforting. For instance, the person who died may have been too ill to express his or her feelings or to say "goodbye" and the relatives also may not have had an opportunity for a final exchange. It is a good chance for both to tie up loose ends and resolve any outstanding questions.*

Mediums link with spirits *mainly through spirit guides that they know and trust. The guides establish contact—but only if the spirits wish to be in communication.*

The spirit of someone who has died *may appear vividly alive to the medium, as if he or she is in the same room; or the medium may sense the person so completely that he/she is able to give a realistic description of the person. The medium also can have two-way conversations with the spirit.*

a compelling desire to be in contact with spirits on the astral level. In this case, it's most important to seek expert guidance. Even if you have an inborn gift for contacting spirits, you can be drawn into subtle, nebulous areas that can create illusions and delusions. Do plenty of research first, and consult a highly recommended spiritualist association, a trained medium, or a reputable psychic development group.

Steps to Mastering Mediumship

A development group under the supervision of a competent medium or teacher is the place in which to work on any innate abilities.

Silence and meditational exercises will be used in order to make individuals more receptive to the currents in the spirit world. The teacher will work with you to help develop your gifts of clairvoyance (see page 90), clairaudience (hearing voices), and clairsentience (see page 58)—all of which come into play when you make yourself a channel for spirits to communicate through.

THE OUIJA BOARD

Many people try to contact departed spirits with the help of a ouija board—this has letters and numbers on it, and a sliding pointer, which spells out messages in response to questions. It can be used by one person or a group. Though it is generally regarded as an entertaining psychic "game," the ouija is a frightening experience for some because it tends to attract lower spirit entities. These have been known to tease and scare people by spelling out worrying messages—including warnings of death or injury. The safest way to use the board is to invoke only the highest and most benevolent spirits before you ask your questions. Prayerful meditation before beginning can create the best atmosphere.

Getting in Touch with Your Spirit Guide

If you've ever wondered whether it's possible for you to initiate communication with a being from the spirit world, the answer is "yes"—but it is often easier to receive help from a spirit guide. Unfortunately, you can easily be led astray in your quest. While Native American chieftains, cosmic brothers from distant galaxies, or famous people from history have all been hailed as the only true spirit guides, the reassuring truth is that a spirit guide or mentor does not have to project a distinct identity. In fact, the most effective ones are the least "personalized," and don't even have names. Essentially, the absence of personality in a guide is the sign of a truly genuine force. Authentic spirit mentors never interfere or intervene in anyone's daily life. No benevolent being would tell you what to do. Your guide's role is to unconditionally advise you. They can also assist you to make contact with the spirit world, directing you wisely and safely.

You can safely link up with a spirit guide as described opposite, as long as you invoke this guidance with trust and goodwill. Alternatively, if you think you'd feel more comfortable doing this with other people, always choose a highly reputable psychic development group.

Are your messages real?

A quick way to check whether you're dealing with an "authentic" spirit is to see whether you agree with the following statements.

There is a distinct feeling of love and wisdom.

Taken out of context, the messages have a general meaning.

The information you received was inspirational and thought-provoking.

If, on the other hand, the list of statements below more accurately reflects your experiences, then you shouldn't take this source seriously.

When messages come through, they refer to personal matters.

The guide has an impressive sounding name.

The guide tells you what to do.

He or she has told you that you were special.

The guide says that its message is vital to save the world.

RECEIVING SPIRIT MESSAGES

Perform the following exercise to connect with the spirit world. Ask a reliable friend to tape the words you receive.

1 *Use the exercise on page 23 to become deeply relaxed, and breathe steadily until you feel fully balanced.*

2 *Powerfully invoke your desire to be linked to the highest forces of good through prayerful meditation. Ask for help to make a clear connection with your guiding spirit.*

3 *Visualize the top of your crown center (see page 29) opening out like a funnel of pure light, and take your consciousness as high as you can. Now take it a little higher, and then raise it even further upward.*

4 *Visualize yourself enveloped from head to toe in a column of pure light. You may be aware that words are filling your head out of nowhere.*

5 *Speak these words out loud as they come to you. If you notice that your attention is wandering, you have broken the link. You can either guide yourself back into communication, or stop, and try again some other time.*

6 *Return to your regular state of awareness by visualizing a taproot of energy leading down into the inner core of the earth.*

7 *Draw on that energy, feeling deep security and pleasure in your physical existence.*

Messages from Beyond

In times of acute crisis or trauma, you may have uttered a desperate but unconscious cry into the universe, begging for an answer to your dilemma. Sometimes, these calls for help trigger a response; it may arrive in the form of a dream, or through some event that turns out to be a "heaven-sent" solution. This is because you have unwittingly achieved a form of pure communication to the higher powers.

You don't necessarily require faith to appeal to them; the ability to be true to your inner self, and remain open to all sources of help, is just as important. Moreover, sheer inspiration can get to the heart of many difficulties, though it often means changing your perspective.

When you're struggling with a dilemma that tests you to your limits, every nerve in your body can feel wired. Ironically, such tension also may make you less receptive to the subtle ways in which messages are delivered. Try and keep part of your mind relaxed and open, so you have the mental space to sense the hidden meaning behind odd words or phrases that arrive "out of the blue." Answers tend to sneak into your mind when you're involved in mundane tasks such as brushing your teeth or driving your car. You can often be more open to inspiration when you're physically occupied. Once you learn to keep an open mind, you'll recognize signals promptly, and trust what you receive.

JUST ASK!

When seeking divine guidance, always make sure you know exactly what you want.

1 *Concentrate on the essence of your question, and formulate the simplest way of expressing it. This helps to generate a positive result.*

2 *If possible, choose a night when the moon is waxing (half way between a new and full moon). Look deep into the night sky, then send your question to the guiding forces of the heavens.*

3 *If you have a dream that night, and recall it when you wake up, write its details in your psychic journal. This could be your answer.*

4 *Otherwise, note any unusual insights that arrive; they will certainly come from a higher source of intuition. Accept these messages without analyzing them too much, even if they don't make sense. In time, their meaning will become clear.*

HOW TO LISTEN

Messages arrive from beyond in a variety of ways. The following are just a few examples.

Key words

You gradually become aware that a single word seems to pop up all the time—in a newspaper headline, on a poster, in a television ad, on a highway sign, even on a food wrapper. As soon as you've realized this, the meaning of that word will be clear.

Images

As with word messages, you'll suddenly notice yourself seeing the same image over and over. This may be something as simple as an arrow pointing in one direction. The moment you acknowledge this, you'll know what the message is saying.

Inspiration

You may feel compelled to take an intuitive leap in the dark and reach for a particular item among many—a fortune cookie, a rune, or a playing or tarot card. Whatever you discover, there is your answer.

Coincidence

Sometimes the message seems to drop in front of you out of the sky—as you're walking along, you see something on the sidewalk. It may be a bird's feather, a coin, or a discarded flower. As soon as you pick the object up, your mind recognizes the message that is being sent.

How to Communicate with Angels

You are surrounded by countless angelic beings who act as messengers between earth and heaven, and link you with the highest good. The most familiar of these is your guardian angel, the protective being that presides over your life from the moment of your birth (see page 160). However, an array of different angels are responsible for delivering the life-changing messages that act as torch-lights in darkness, and provide higher guidance, healing, and protection.

You may have been living from day to day without a particular sense of purpose, unaware of these mighty angels who are particularly concerned about your personal destiny. They can see the path you need to follow for your ultimate spiritual fulfilment; moreover, if you know how to "ask," they will help you to find your way, and restore you to your spiritual roots.

Angels are known to prefer quiet, spiritual atmospheres; with this in mind, reserve a special place in your home, and introduce some of the elements described below. Ideally, this will be also the place where you meditate regularly.

Angels always act in a spirit of unconditional love—they will unfailingly point you toward your true destination, stimulating your mind and imagination, sharpening your perception of the world, and supporting your instinct to do good. They also can bring you dazzling insights—and a sense of true enlightenment that will enhance your psychic creativity.

A WELCOMING ATMOSPHERE

The qualities that most appeal to angels include:

Calm
Regular meditation brings you inner quiet and peace, and this permeates the space around you.

Candlelight
Light a candle every day—its steady flame will attract quiet, gentle illumination into your life.

Cleanliness
Always keeping your meditation space tidy and dirt free.

Simplicity
Keep your space clear and uncluttered.

Joy
What makes you happy?
Is it music, a picture, or an exquisite shell? Use and enjoy these in your meditation space—angels love happiness, and are said to dance on the vibrations of your laughter.

Many people have actually seen angels—usually at times of great crisis. One of the most famous sightings was witnessed by soldiers on the battlefield at Mons, in France, during the 1914–18 war. In the midst of the slaughter, a huge, radiant being appeared, giving comfort and love to the wounded and dying; it was the legendary Angel of Mons.

There are several common factors in eyewitness descriptions of angels: the overwhelming impact is that of a tall, shining presence that is so bright, it dazzles the eye. The streams of light that emanate from these androgenous beings appear to be wing-like forms, and the emotional projection is one of great strength, reassurance, and profound love. Angelic forces rarely speak in words, but the messages they bring penetrate directly into human consciousness, and are clearly understood.

At any time of your life, you can appeal to the archangels for guidance, even though you may never see one. You must know how to ask, however, and this means being clear about what is going wrong in your life. You may feel adrift in your career, or in your relationships, or you may have no sense of inner peace. Take some time to focus these concerns around the different strengths offered by each archangel—they are the messengers who will respond most directly to your problems. Clear your mind and compose your thoughts in your psychic journal; and trust your intuition to lead you to the angel that can help you most at this point in your life. Then, approach your chosen angel through the avenues suggested here—those of meditation, and prayer.

THE ARCHANGELS

Gabriel
The messenger of divine comfort, Gabriel represents female power. Gabriel announced the coming of Christ and is thought to be the messanger who dictated the Koran. This is the angel to invoke to help with fertility problems; the archangel also brings news.

Metatron
This heavenly scribe has many eyes and records everything that happens; his key task is to reunite male and female principles. His name means "mentor," and he is the angel to invoke when you seek spiritual teaching and guidance.

Michael
With his mighty sword of truth, Michael stands for justice, and springs to the defense of the weak and downtrodden. When you're at your lowest ebb, ask for his courage, fortitude, and integrity. He will help you to defeat any terrifying elements that haunt your life.

Raphael
Turn to Raphael when you are feeling ill; he will bring you a deeply regenerative energy that can restore you to health.

Raquel
The angel of ethical procedure, Raquel monitors all aspects of behavior. Invoke him when you are seeking justice and the right course of action—he will help you to make those difficult choices in your life.

Saraquel
This is the teacher of Moses—a fallen angel who then repented. If you feel that you've done wrong and seek forgiveness, turn to him to restore you to your peace of mind.

Uriel
The angel of enlightenment and the upholder of moral teaching, Uriel misses nothing, and is a steadfast doorkeeper. His energy is uncompromising, he will always "tell it like it is." Appeal to him when you feel mentally overwhelmed and confused.

ANGELIC MEDITATION

Let your chosen archangel bring you messages in the stillness of meditation.

1 *Focus on your breathing as described on page 23, and let yourself become perfectly serene and still inside. If you wish, you can hold a picture of the archangel you have chosen, or a card inscribed with the angel's name.*

2 *Now shift your attention to your heart center, and open yourself completely and trustingly to the archangel's loving presence.*

3 *Allow any form of communication from the angel to enter your consciousness freely; accept, trust, and absorb what you are given in the spirit of truth.*

4 *Remain in quiet contact with the angel until you feel that you have thoroughly absorbed its guidance at every level of your being; then return to your normal state of awareness.*

REACH OUT TO YOUR ANGEL

Talk to your angel in simple words spoken from the heart.

1 *Choose the angel who can help you most—for instance, if you're feeling bullied and intimidated by more forceful people, Michael can help you. Think how you would talk to a trusted friend when asking for advice, then imagine that you are addressing Michael in the same way. Write your words down in the form of a brief letter.*

2 *For example, you could say, "Dear Michael, I'm so frightened, and uncertain all the time. I let people walk all over me, and I've lost all confidence in myself. Please help me to find my inner strength, and protect me from all my fears. Thank you for knowing what I'm going through, and for standing up for people like me who have lost their courage. The feeling that you're always on my side is a true comfort."*

3 *At bedtime, calm your thoughts and trust that your angel is ready to come to you. Then either read your prayer silently or say it out loud, knowing that your words are being heard and understood.*

4 *A good night's sleep, after which you awaken rested and confident, may be a sign your prayer was heard. Or you can always "ask" for a more concrete response (see above).*

Can You Identify Different Spirits?

Have you ever met a ghost? Those who've had first-hand experience describe remarkably similar sensations: the sudden feeling of extreme cold, an unpleasant odor, and an unsettling sense that something is very amiss. A ghostly form is simply a non-physical manifestation of someone who is dead. Many old houses claim to have a ghost-in-residence. One example might be a spectral presence that walks on the staircase at certain times. Beings such as these are earthbound spirits; they have failed to move on to the astral or spirit world because, for some reason, they are unable to leave their familiar home ground. There is some evidence that they can be helped to move on (see below).

A poltergeist, or "noisy spirit," is quite a different matter. It gets up to all sorts of mischief, moving objects around, breaking things and making violent, loud noises. It certainly wants to be noticed, whereas ghosts are usually shy and elusive.

The latest evidence suggests that, far from being a spirit presence, a poltergeist may manifest from the disturbed energy of a living person. One often appears in the home of a young person who is emotionally disturbed; he or she may be completely unaware of having any connection with the mysterious noises and activity. Fortunately, once any hidden problems are acknowledged and treated, the poltergeist usually goes away.

FREEING A GHOST

Rescuing an earthbound being demands great love, and freedom from fear.

1 *Using your breath as a focus, meditate on the unity of all life, as described on page 23. Know that, as you breathe, everything else breathes.*

2 *Now focus on your heart center, and visualize it opening out like a giant blossom, basking in sunlight. With each in-breath, take the sun's warmth and healing energy deep into your cells, to the core of your being.*

3 *With each out-breath, share this warmth with everything around you, without exception.*

4 *Now ask the angelic forces of love to come to you, and welcome them inside your heart. Feel them repairing and healing your aura, wrapping you inside a powerful energy field of protection and strength.*

5 *At this point you can communicate with the ghost or spirit energy; if you feel the time is right, lovingly suggest that it moves into the realms of light.*

6 *The spirit will only respond positively to being liberated when you are completely free of fear yourself. If you have the smallest doubt, do not intervene; you should never approach a spirit alone, and without strengthening yourself in advance.*

What spirit is there?

If you're not certain of the nature of the spirit you've encountered, look at the statements below. If you agree with the first three:

❏ Objects get thrown around or move on their own;
❏ There are sudden thuds or other unexplained noises;
❏ The spirit seems to know how to make you angry;

This would indicate poltergeist activity, so you should check whether someone in the house is suffering from a hidden psychological disturbance.

If, on the other hand, the following statements are more indicative of the spirit's behavior:

❏ The presence always appears at the same time;
❏ The activity is always in the same place;
❏ The spirit is apparently unaware of your presence;
❏ You feel that you vaguely recognize the being;
❏ The atmosphere suddenly becomes very cold;

Then the presence is most likely to be a ghost. If the ghost is upsetting your life, and you want it to leave, you might try to set it free yourself. But this should only be attempted when you are psychically strong; if you have any doubt, ask for help from a trained medium recommended by a spiritualist group, or a priest trained in exorcism.

PSYCHIC PROTECTION 6

How Strong is Your Aura?

When you balance your chakras as described on page 31, you strengthen your aura by activating levels of pure energy deep inside yourself. As a result, the harmony restored to your mind, body, and spirit is reflected in a strong, clear, shining aura. This shows that you have the psychic energy to live your life to the full, and you radiate an almost tangible glow of inner security and confidence. Sadly, however, this strength won't last if you haven't corrected the more negative traits and imbalances in your character—your aura will inevitably revert back to its weaker, unhealthier state.

Psychic healing and enhanced intuition can certainly transform your life—but only if you help the process along. Do this by building up your store of self-knowledge; keep regular notes in your psychic journal, acknowledging and accepting your particular weaknesses and strengths with candor and good humor. Try to correct your negative habits, but most important of all, reach out for any opportunities to

How strong are you?

Look at the questions below and tick the ones that relate to you.

When you have a disagreement with anyone, do you drop any negative feelings:
- ❏ **a** Within minutes.
- ❏ **b** 24 hours.
- ❏ **c** Several days or even weeks.

When you're talking to someone who is in a bad mood or distressed, do you:
- ❏ **a** Maintain your own equilibrium.
- ❏ **b** Let that person's pain affect you.
- ❏ **c** Feel drained afterwards.

When you visit a friend who is sick or in the hospital do you:
- ❏ **a** Know you can bring a positive atmosphere with you.
- ❏ **b** Feel slightly uneasy around anyone who's ill.
- ❏ **c** Become unwell yourself.

When someone compliments you, do you:
- ❏ **a** Say "Thank you!" but pay little attention.
- ❏ **b** Feel embarrassed and turn the compliment back.
- ❏ **c** Glow with pleasure and tell everyone.

If you someone criticizes you, do you:
- ❏ **a** Acknowledge that there is some truth in it, and try to adjust any imbalances to your character accordingly.
- ❏ **b** Fire back some negative words.
- ❏ **c** Spend days, or even weeks, brooding about it.

change your life for the better, rather than pretending that you don't have any problems.

However, much as you try to bolster your aura with healing, visualization, and balancing work, any persistent weak spots will be revealed there. You can identify some of these by answering the questions below; don't be discouraged—you'll discover your positive qualities there as well.

If you answered...

❏ Mostly a's

You are very centered in your own energy—this is a good basis for maintaining your psychic health.

❏ Mostly b's

You respond naturally to the input around you and are highly sympathetic, but you need to develop a stronger sense of autonomy. Use visualization and meditation to help with this.

❏ Mostly c's

Faced with other people's opinions and moods you are easily shaken and put off-balance. Seek help and skilled healing to restore your inner balance.

Emergency action

However robust you are normally, situations can suddenly overwhelm your inner resources. Here are three examples of how to get yourself out of trouble:

When talking to a distressed friend, you may realize that, while he or she is obviously feeling better by the minute, you are becoming totally exhausted. This is easy to rectify: simply fold your arms across your solar plexus—this prevents you from "bleeding" psychic energy.

You may suddenly find yourself in a threatening situation, for instance, when you're walking alone at night. If this happens, visualize a powerful golden light all around you. This often has the effect of making you invisible to others.

If you're having a lot of trouble with someone—parent, child or colleague, for example—visualize yourself in a clear bubble of white light. Spend several moments just being comfortable and happy inside. Then, conjure up an image of the person with whom you are having problems. Now imagine that person in his or her own separate bubble of light. Draw a figure of eight between them, then visualise cutting apart the two bubbles and watch the other person's bubble gently float away. Implement this exercise in a detached manner. Performed correctly this is a powerful healing tool.

Amulets and Talismans

Do you have a special mascot that makes you feel safe and strong, or always brings you luck? If so, you're part of a psychic tradition that is as old as humanity itself; this recognizes that certain objects either have powerful qualities in themselves, or can be endowed for a particular purpose.

These potent items fall into two groups—amulets and talismans—but they equip you with extra psychic strength in different ways. An amulet is protective in its action, and diverts evil influences from the owner; its traditional purpose is to ward off the "evil eye," the common phrase used when someone is directing negative energy at you.

Amulets may repel danger, but they don't necessarily attract luck. This is the role of the talisman—a special charm with the power to bring you good fortune. Charm bracelets remain a popular item today. They enable the wearer to amass a collection of tiny objects, some acting as amulets,

The best way to protect yourself from negative energies is to keep your aura strong and healthy as described on page 156. But if you are intuitively drawn to an object because it makes you feel particularly good, follow your instincts. Keep your mascot close to you at all times; you could wear it on a chain around your neck, on a key ring, hang it in your car, or keep it safely hidden away in your purse or wallet. Its presence will reassure you, and give you a sense of extra good fortune and protection.

"Abracadabra" *Used by magicians all over the world, this is one of the oldest magic formulas, and means "Speak the blessing." Written on a piece of silk, and worn around the neck, it wards off disease.*

Beads *Glass eye-beads represent the "all seeing" deity that averts danger.*

Cat *The ancient Egyptians believed cats were sacred, and represented the moon. Black cats are thought to be lucky, but some people fear them. Only you will know whether a cat mascot will benefit you, so trust your intuition.*

Coin *This is traditionally silver, but if it's the right coin for you, the humble penny will bring you health and wealth.*

**Crosses—
Ankh or key cross** *This originated in Egypt and symbolizes life and immortality.*

Greek cross, or the cross of St Benedict *Both these crosses send off evil spirits with the commanding message "Get thee behind me Satan!"*

Roman cross *This was a powerful protective amulet long before Christianity.*
St Andrew's cross *Traditionally worn as a potent amulet against bad influences.*
Tau cross *Shaped like a "T" and worn to protect against diseases such as epilepsy. It is symbolic of eternal life and is also used to guard the spirit.*

Dragon *Usually used to enhance peace and felicity, dragons also help the wearer to conquer enemies in war— you must choose how to use its power.*

Fish *The symbol of early Christianity, fish charms attract abundance and riches, and represent creation and fertility.*

Four-leafed clover or shamrock *These are very lucky plants, renowned for bringing you luck, whether it's in money, gambling, or love.*

Frog *A talisman for wealth, fertility, health, and long life, frog charms should be worn by lovers to ensure a happy relationship, blessed with mutual ardor and constancy.*

Garment *Any piece of clothing can bring the wearer luck—especially in competitive sports. Football players often have "lucky" socks, and some tennis players wear the same shirt throughout a tournament.*

Hand of Fatima *A powerful amulet, this is very popular in the Middle East. It is a hand of benediction, and is mainly used on the doors or walls of the house to protect all within.*

Heart *This is usually worn to attract love and joy. At one time, however, a heart amulet was used to prevent evil spells being used on the wearer.*

Horseshoe *The ancient Greeks and Romans used these to bring wealth and happiness to the home. To make it effective, the horseshoe must be nailed onto the door of the house pointing upward.*

Key *Worn by the Greeks and Romans to bring luck, enhance foresight, and improve judgement, keys represented the god Janus, keeper of the gate of heaven and guardian of all doors. Janus was two-headed, and this enabled him to look into the future as well as the past. The Japanese use a key charm to bring wealth, love, and happiness.*

Lamb *The Christian emblem of the Redeemer, a lamb carrying a cross and flag is worn as a protection against accidents, storms, and diseases.*

Lizard *Painted on the outside of houses, a lizard brings good luck. It also promotes good eyesight and inspires wisdom.*

Lotus *This brings good luck, and is also used in India as an amulet to protect against illness and accidents. The flower represents Lakshmi, the goddess of beauty and fortune. The Egyptians saw the lotus as an emblem of the sun, and believed that it promoted clarity of thought and wisdom.*

Peacock *The feathers are said to bring bad luck as they are supposed to represent the evil eye. However, the bird itself is lucky, and represents the triumph over death of everlasting life.*

Rabbit's foot *With its associations of fertility and speed, this lucky charm boosts your fortunes.*

Scarab *This ancient Egyptian talisman is a symbol of creation and resurrection, and brings physical, spiritual, and mental health. It also acts as a protection from evil influences on the journey from the physical to the spirit planes.*

Seal of Solomon *Also known as the Star of David. It symbolizes the fire of the male and the water of the female merging in harmony. The crossed triangles also represent air and earth. The seal has six points, with an invisible seventh representing spiritual transformation, reflected within the inner eye of the magician, seer, priest, or priestess.*

Spider *A talisman of success in business and money matters, spiders were placed inside a nutshell in medieval times, and worn around the neck to protect the wearer from illness.*

Teeth *In China a tiger's tooth is regarded as a precious talisman for people who gamble or speculate. In Russia imitation teeth are used as amulets to protect children from evil influences and diseases.*

Tortoise *The symbol of the earth, this protects against spells and various evil spirits.*

White heather *This Celtic talisman has the power to bring true love to the wearer.*

Wishbone *This familiar talisman brings you good luck and enables you to realize your dreams.*

Meeting Your Guardian Angel

The moment you were born, you automatically acquired a powerful source of psychic protection—your guardian angel. Many psychics believe that the same protective being accompanies you through many lifetimes, seeing you safely through each stage of your soul's journey toward spiritual enlightenment.

On a day-to-day basis, your guardian angel watches over you at all times, and acts as an "invisible mender," constantly repairing and healing subtle areas of damage within your aura. This loving spiritual presence also protects you while you sleep, and wards off negative forces.

You may not even be aware that you have a guardian angel until something happens to trigger you into psychic contact—usually at a moment of emotional crisis. When this happens, the experience is unforgettable; it is the deep, intuitive recognition of unconditional love.

It could also be the first step in learning how to communicate with your guardian angel on a positive basis. However, this requires intelligent collaboration from you; your angel will certainly guide, heal, and protect you, but that does not mean that you can avoid taking responsibility for your own actions.

Communication guidelines

Acknowledge the presence of your angel by your welcoming words and behavior.

Choose a regular time to communicate with your guardian angel—many people do this at night before going to sleep.

Always ask for help in clear, simple terms.

If you are troubled with bad dreams or negative feelings, ask your guardian angel to protect you.

Remain open to messages from your angel at all times, especially if you sense that you are being warned of danger.

Don't be reckless with your personal safety—your guardian angel is there to protect you, but can't override your free will.

INVOKING YOUR GUARDIAN ANGEL

1 *Focus on your breathing until you become fully relaxed, as described on page 23.*

2 *Breathing gently into the heart center, quietly ask your guardian angel to come close and make itself known to you.*

3 *Allow the angel to surround you with its healing energy, and feel yourself enfolded within gently caressing wings.*

4 *Let yourself relax completely into this warmth, and ask for any help that you may need.*

5 *Quietly absorb the responsive energy until you are completely satisfied. Although the angel does not require thanks, you'll feel a compelling need to express your gratitude.*

6 *Return to your regular state of physical awareness, and carry the sense of unconditional love with you into the rest of your day.*

HIGHER CONSCIOUSNESS

7

The Mystic Way

Mysticism—whereby the individual aims to achieve direct intuitive experience of the divine—exists both within all major religions and outside in the form of personal spiritual practices. It is not an easy spiritual pathway; the mystic must first discover his or her "real" self in order to make direct contact with the Godhead—the ultimate, eternal, source of love.

If you want to become a mystic, you have to work at dissolving all the personality traits that obscure this true self. These are the complicated "veils of illusion," "masks," or "cloaks" that you use to conceal your inner identity, and they all can get in the way of achieving pure spiritual communication.

The best way to overcome this barrier is through honesty and regular meditation (see page 23); this will help you to confront who you really are; a true knowledge of your real self is often regarded as the highest form of intuition. Meditation may not bring you total enlightenment, but it can give you an authentic inner directive—and offers you a more fulfilling way to focus your existence. Being more focused helps you to get in touch with the universal forces of the cosmos. When this happens, you will find sublime peace from experiencing the mystical unity of all life; you'll realize that everything is inextricably linked, and that you are a single, living drop in the limitless ocean of creation. This hints at a wonderful truth shining through all living things, and inspires a unique sense of love and wonder.

Are you a natural mystic?

Give the following questions careful thought, then check those to which you have an affirmative response. At the end, add up how many you checked.

❏ Do you sometimes "know" exactly what to do?

❏ Are you actively involved in psychic self-development?

❏ Do you seek the truth?

❏ Have you ever felt that all human beings are connected in some way?

❏ Even at times of great material success, or after winning a much sought-after goal, do you sense that this is not all there is to life?

❏ Can you stand up for what you believe in, even if it goes against everyone else?

- ❏ Are you able to take a different direction to the rest of your group/family/peers, if it feels right for you?
- ❏ At times of great crisis or chaos, are you able to see beyond immediate events to some greater illumination?
- ❏ Do you always carry out what you promise, even when you don't feel like doing it?
- ❏ Do you make extra efforts to do tasks that others feel are unnecessary?
- ❏ Do you have an inclusive love of other human beings?
- ❏ Do you love yourself?
- ❏ Can you pick yourself up after disappointments, whatever they are, and carry on regardless?
- ❏ Are you very happy to be in your own company?
- ❏ Can you sense spiritual aspirations in others?

Assessment

❏ **2–3**
Even if you only checked 2 or 3 questions, you already have some mystical traits.

❏ **4–10**
You are walking toward a spiritual destination, even if you are not aware of it at this moment in time.

❏ **11–15**
You are consciously on the road toward mystical union with the ultimate truth and spiritual illumination.

What is Your Karma?

Roughly understood as fate, karma is something we can affect. The law of karma says that every thought and feeling that you direct onto others, at any time, will react on you in equal measure. Our karma evolves through many past lives, but also operates in the here and now—at every second of your existence. You are the sum total of all your experiences over all lifetimes, and this is reflected in your life today. This means that you are completely responsible for your actions, and that you can choose to change your karma for the better at any moment during your life.

Your soul is your true essence, and each incarnation gives it a chance to experience, learn, and grow within a different physical body. In this way, you can perceive the karmic laws of cause and effect over several lifetimes, circumstances, and situations. Karma is all-pervasive and powerful, yet it is also fair and compassionate; you can't escape its relentless lessons, but it is a force that attracts exactly what you need for your soul to progress.

So, whatever is happening in your life, good or bad, consider how each event relates to your karmic destiny: from this viewpoint, it is impossible to be in the wrong place at the wrong time.

Instant retribution

One day, after driving around for ages, I spotted a vacant parking space and drove ahead a little to give myself room to reverse back into it. Then, out of nowhere, another car slipped into my space. I got really mad, and directed a volley of unpleasant thoughts onto the driver with some force. I immediately realized that I had sent out very destructive energy, and tried to retrieve it as best I could.

The next day, as I was parking in another part of town, a car drew up alongside me; the driver yelled and shouted, claiming that I had stolen his place. He was in a terrible rage, and even threatened to drive into my car. I was scared and perplexed, as I had not seen him waiting. People gathered around, and I got out of my car to call his bluff; eventually he drove away, leaving me very shaken. Suddenly, I recognized that this violent energy was the very same one that I had expressed the previous day.

A KARMIC SEARCH

Use this exploratory visualization to identify your karmic path.

1 *Focus your breathing as described on page 23, until you feel completely relaxed. Now open yourself to any images and sensations that have always had a particular meaning for you. For instance, you may have an instinctive love for a language, place, building, or landscape.*

2 *Or, you may have unusually strong aversions; for no evident reason, you may find that you react violently to an animal, a uniform, a color, or odor. This may be connected with the cause of your last death—especially if you're abnormally terrified of fire or knives.*

3 *Allow these images to float into your mind without trying to rationalize them. This will allow you to reconnect with the deepest areas of your life naturally and intuitively.*

4 *Gradually, you'll make the creative link with your essential self—the core identity that threads its way through time. You may suddenly recognize an image originating from eons past that is eerily familiar to you at this very moment. You are seeing yourself, traveling along your karmic path.*

Channeling Spiritual Messages

People who act as channels for spiritual information from the highest sources of knowledge practice a specialized form of mediumship. Regular mediums (see page 142) communicate with discarnate spirits—the souls of those who have died and inhabit the astral plane—whereas channelers deliver information from more impersonal contacts. These more impersonal contacts include spirits who have completed their round of earthly incarnations, the higher spirit guides, and the Ascended Masters, who have journeyed beyond the soul.

Channeling can bring profound rewards; it is both a means of access to cosmic information, and a gateway that takes you into other dimensions. However, to achieve meaningful results, the integrity of your motivation is paramount. Your aim is to align yourself with the most authentic, trusted and benign sources: this takes intelligence, clarity of thought, and dedicated work on self-awareness and healing.

Before you attempt the channeling exercise described on page 171, you should answer the questionnaire below, to discover whether you are ready to proceed.

Are you ready to channel?

If you respond "yes" to a question, check the box next to it. Add up the checks and note your score.

What is your motive for wanting to bring through channeled material?

- ❏ **a** To obtain inspirational knowledge.
- ❏ **b** To expand your own awareness.
- ❏ **c** So others will respect you, or pay more attention to you.

Describe your physical constitution:

- ❏ **a** You are rarely ill.
- ❏ **b** You commonly suffer from colds and other minor illnesses.
- ❏ **c** You often visit doctors, healers, or pharmacies.

What sort of reading material do you favor?

- ❏ **a** Sensational stories.
- ❏ **b** Information covering a wide variety of topics.
- ❏ **c** Escapist romantic novels.

How much time are you prepared to spend on developing yourself as a clear channel?

- ❏ **a** When you feel like it.
- ❏ **b** However many years it may take.
- ❏ **c** Maybe once a week for an hour or two.

Are you someone who is:

- ❏ **a** Fearless.
- ❏ **b** Rarely frightened about anything.
- ❏ **c** Always watchful, expecting bad things to happen.

Assessment

❏ **3–5 c's**

You would be much better suited to some other form of psychic or healing work.

❏ **3–5 a's**

You seem to have some unrealistic ideas about yourself, and you need to engage in more self discovery and healing before becoming involved in channeling.

❏ **3–5 b's**

You show great promise, and could develop your channeling abilities very nicely, with dedication and purpose.

In recent years channeling has been widely used, but the quality of the messages varies enormously. Some warn of alarming changes to our planet, often in sensationalized, frightening terms. Other revelations have a core of authentic insight that are encouraging radical shifts in spiritual awareness. Always retain a discerning attitude to this information.

If you decide to try channeling, you should realize that this involves entering a focused state. As you may not remember the content of what has been directed through you, ask a trusted friend to tape or write down the messages that you receive.

Channeled information

When channeling comes into actuality through the spoken word, it permeates through the mind of all humanity, and creates an energy of realisation. Although this spiritual journey is never easy, the rewards are great.

"He may travel sometimes in the dark, and the illusion of darkness is very real. He may travel sometimes in a light so dazzling and bewildering that he can scarcely see the way ahead. He may know what it is to falter on the path and to drop under the fatigue of service and of strife, be temporarily distracted and wander down the bypaths of ambition, or self-interest and of material enchantment. But the lapse will be but brief. Nothing in heaven or hell, on earth or elsewhere can prevent the progress of the man who has awakened to the illusion, who has glimpsed the reality, beyond the glamour of the astral plane."

Alice Bailey, *A Treatise on White Magic*

ALIGNMENT TO LIGHT

1 *To prepare yourself for channeling, avoid eating a heavy meal beforehand, and allow at least two hours before you begin this procedure.*

2 *Follow the meditation exercise on page 23, and take plenty of time to achieve a deeply relaxed state.*

3 *Focus your energy into your heart center. Hold it there, breathing regularly and deeply for at least three breaths.*

4 *Visualize a giant, diamond crystal poised above your head, and invoke the highest sources of divine spiritual consciousness.*

5 *Watch and acknowledge pure energy pouring into the crystal. Feel and hear the frequency of light vibrating through it.*

6 *At this point you may feel a responsive humming sound building up inside you—sing this sound out into the space around you.*

7 *Visualize the light being split into rainbow colors, and radiating from the crystal directly into your higher centers. Absorb these rays.*

8 *Let your mind become completely open and free—and don't think. Allow words to come into your mind, and speak them out loud without listening to what you are saying. This takes some practice, but you will learn to assess whether it is an authentic message.*

9 *When your channeling link has ended, return to your normal state. Make sure that you concentrate on your feet, and feel a strong root of energy linking them to the earth.*

10 *After completing this exercise, go for a walk and eat a solid meal with a hot drink.*

Index

Acknowledgments

Author acknowledgments

Many grateful thanks go to: the dedicated team at Carroll & Brown; Derek Hawkins for his assistance in the Astrology page; and my husband Rupert, both for assistance with the healing section, and for his continuous loving support.

For more information on the School of Insight and Intuition see www.insightandintuition.com

Carroll & Brown would like to thank:

Additional design assistance *Roland Codd, Emily Cook, Justin Ford*

Additional editorial assistance *Tom Broder*

Illustrations *Jürgen Ziewe*
(pages 30–1, 34–5, 73, 140–1, 145, 160–1)

Production Manager *Karol Davies*

Production Controller *Nigel Reed*

Computer Management *Paul Stradling*

Picture Researcher *Sandra Schneider*

Indexer *Madeline Weston*

Picture credits

page **9** Getty Images; page **15** (left) Jules Selmes; page **27** AUM, digital image by Judith Cornell Ph.D., award-winning author of *Mandala: Luminous Symbols for Healing*, www.mandala-universe.com; page **32** (left) Telegraph Colour Library, (second left) Art Wolfe/SPL; page **40** Museo Dali, Figueras, Spain/Index/Bridgeman Art Library ©Salvador Dali, Gala-Salvador Dali Foundation,DACS, London 2001; page **42** Manfred Kage/Science Photo Library; page **75** Sue Baker/Science Photo Library; page **86** The Charles Walker Collection; page **87** The Charles Walker Collection; page **112** Elgin and Hall, customer helpline 01677 450100 www.elgin.co.uk; page **143** Getty Images; page **147** (second left) Jules Selmes; page **149** Profile by Odilon Redon 1840–1916, Christies/Bridgeman Art Library; page **170–1** David Parker/Science Photo Library

Text credit

page **170** A. Baily, A Treatise on White Magic (Lucius Press)

Every effort has been made to trace the copyright holders of the back cover image (right), and also pages 162, 167. We apologize in advance for any omissions and would be pleased to insert the appropriate acknowledgment in any subsequent edition of this publication.